'Communication becomes a core disorders who often cry: "You do not listen." This book bridges this gulf.'

— *Professor Janet Treasure, King's College, London*

'Eating disorders are very effective at getting the most rational individual to think in the most irrational of ways. This is confusing to the sufferer and those who attempt to care for the patient, be they parents or professionals. This book will help us all understand these perplexing disorders just a little better.'

— *Professor Daniel Le Grange, University of Chicago*

'One of the most difficult aspects of an eating disorder is the way the illness distorts anything and everything that's said to the sufferer. This book will help expose those distortions in a simple but highly effective way. An important read for both clinicians and families.'

— *Harriet Brown, author of* Brave Girl Eating:
A Family's Struggle with Anorexia

# Ed says U said

*of related interest*

**A Parent's Guide to Defeating Eating Disorders**
**Spotting the Stealth Bomber and Other Symbolic Approaches**
*Ahmed Boachie and Karin Jasper*
*Foreword by Dr. Debra Katzman*
ISBN 978 1 84905 196 5
eISBN 978 0 85700 528 1

**Maintaining Recovery from Eating Disorders**
**Avoiding Relapse and Recovering Life**
*Naomi Feigenbaum*
*Foreword by Rebekah Bardwell Doweyko*
ISBN 978 1 84905 815 5
eISBN 978 0 85700 250 1

**One Life**
**Hope, Healing and Inspiration on the Path to**
**Recovery from Eating Disorders**
*Naomi Feigenbaum*
ISBN 978 1 84310 912 9
eISBN 978 1 84642 947 7

**Beating Eating Disorders Step by Step**
**A Self-Help Guide for Recovery**
*Anna Paterson*
ISBN 978 1 84310 340 0
eISBN 978 1 84642 759 6

**Anorexics on Anorexia**
*Edited by Rosemary Shelley*
ISBN 978 1 85302 471 9
eISBN 978 1 84642 845 6

**Bulimics on Bulimia**
*Edited by Maria Stavrou*
ISBN 978 1 84310 668 5
eISBN 978 1 84642 845 6

# Ed says U said

## Eating Disorder Translator

June Alexander and Cate Sangster

Foreword by Laura Collins

Afterword by Susan Ringwood

Jessica Kingsley *Publishers*
London and Philadelphia

First published in 2013
by Jessica Kingsley Publishers
116 Pentonville Road
London N1 9JB, UK
and
400 Market Street, Suite 400
Philadelphia, PA 19106, USA

*www.jkp.com*

**Library of Congress Cataloging in Publication Data**
Alexander, June, 1950-
Ed says U said : the eating disorder translator / June Alexander and Cate Sangster ; foreword
by Laura Collins ; afterword by Susan Ringwood.
p. cm.
Includes index.
ISBN 978-1-84905-331-0 (alk. paper)
1. Eating disorders--Psychological aspects. 2. Eating disorders--Treatment. 3. Eating disorders
in children--Patients--Family relationships. 4. Eating disorders in adolescence--Patients--Family
relationships. 5. Parent and child. 6. Parent and teenager. I. Sangster, Cate. II. Title. III. Title:
Ed says you said.
RJ506.E18A44 2013
616.85'2600835--dc23
2012027365

**British Library Cataloguing in Publication Data**
A CIP catalogue record for this book is available from the British Library

ISBN 978 1 84905 331 0
eISBN 978 0 85700 677 6

Printed and bound in Great Britain

This book is for my grandchildren, Lachlan, Ashton, Olivia, Kayla and Amelia.

*– June Alexander*

For my GP – who always knows the right thing to say even when I misunderstand her.

*– Cate Sangster*

# Contents

# Foreword

The day I realized my daughter had an eating disorder, I thought I already knew all I needed to know about such things. The first lesson was how wrong I had been.

Eating disorders are not what I thought from hearing about them through movies and popular media. Eating disorders are not, I discovered, like any other disorder or issue. I had to learn a new vocabulary, new science and a new way of parenting in a crisis I never imagined having to face. I was in turn frightened, bewildered, frustrated and terribly humbled by what our dear daughter was experiencing and what we were called on to do to help her.

I was a stranger in a very strange land.

This new land comes with a new language as well: the language of Ed. As our family set out toward supporting our dear child, we had to learn to translate the language of Ed into understanding of her experience. We also had to learn in what ways Ed was translating our words and actions – and take care to communicate in a way that was most helpful.

Ed is a skilful linguist, we found. Ed was clever in how he turned good intentions into negatives. He made fear sound angry, and made love appear harsh. His survival depended on dividing the family and separating our daughter from her friends and her favourite activities.

But Ed wasn't that smart, really. Once we understood his patterns, we found that *we* could adjust while he could not. We learned to see through Ed to our beloved child and to know when we were hearing her voice – ever louder, ever stronger – as she did her heroic work to recover.

But at first, this language was not only alien, but also mocked reality. We heard seemingly heartfelt explanations for disordered behaviours. We tried to listen and respect the desires of a young woman who had always until then shown great insight and self-knowledge. I wish someone had handed me then a way to translate Ed. *Ed says U said: Eating Disorder Translator* is that tool.

When someone we love has an eating disorder, it is easy to think there are only two voices in the room: your voice and their voice. But someone else is there that you cannot always hear and often it is that voice that is guiding the conversation. Loving families can be excused for their confusion but cannot afford to misunderstand or, worse, be used by that voice to further isolate and fail our loved one.

I have the great honour to head an international organization of parents of eating disorder patients. My job allows me to walk alongside many families as they negotiate the harrowing task of identifying and participating in treatment. I am often amazed at the moments of new understanding in parents who are perplexed by Ed.

One of my early moments of clarity was the day I left the dinner table to get some salt for my meal. We tried never to leave the table, of course, to help our daughter be supported in her meal. It was less than a minute to the kitchen and back but when I returned, the dog looked happy and my daughter looked angry. I suddenly realized that some of the precious nourishment my daughter needed had gone to a Labrador's bottomless stomach and that the anger I saw was really fear: I had failed to stay nearby where I was needed.

June Alexander and Cate Sangster have honoured the true voice of loved ones and friends with eating disorders by translating their spoken words and nonverbal messages. They've done so with respect and great insight. Also translated here are the ways our words can be heard by those suffering from an eating disorder. What is remarkable is the authors' ability to decode Ed's language in a matter-of-fact way: without pity, without objectification, and with optimism.

I am struck by these words, on p.27: 'A carer is not defined by who they are but by what they do.' And what we can do, alongside the practical tasks of treatment, is hear one another as clearly as possible.

Optimism is the perfect companion to these translations: with understanding comes not only a clear view but also a clearer path. We *can* understand one another and we can communicate even while struggling with the hard work of the recovery process. That understanding serves us well as we go toward that goal and helps us hold our positive, confident view of the future. Optimism, and truly hearing our suffering loved one, are two of the most powerful contributions to recovery.

'But stay strong in the knowledge that the view from the top is magnificent. It's worth every tear' (p.27).

We've been hearing the voice of Ed for a while now in the books and popular media around eating disorders. Many moving memoirs tell the real story of the silent suffering of Ed. What we have not heard enough of is how the voice we hear and the thoughts underneath are often at odds. We are only hearing a little of the thoughts and less still of the thinking behind it.

*Ed says U said: Eating Disorder Translator* is packed with translation from those who know the language of the illness best. This book is a guided tour not of the torturer, but of the sufferer inside.

Strangely, we find that the voice of Ed is international. Universal, but of course still unique to that person. As recovery progresses we are able to see that uniqueness and fluency anew. My delight in and respect for those who have overcome an eating disorder is immense. I believe as we all grow more fluent in what Ed says U said we will also see new narratives, new insights from these wonderful well people.

I look forward to those stories, those travelogues, and the world of compassion and connection that this book of translations will help us to read.

*Laura Collins*

*Executive Director*
*F.E.A.S.T.*
*(Families Empowered and Supporting Treatment of Eating Disorders)*
*www.feast-ed.org*

# Acknowledgements

We have many people to thank for the content in this book. First and foremost are the people who courageously and generously offered to share their experience with an eating disorder.

Carers come in many forms and we have mothers, fathers, brothers, sisters, grandparents and friends all kindly providing eating disorder dialogues to lighten the load of others who find themselves on the same road.

At the same time, sufferers across the spectrum and age range of eating disorders candidly describe their innermost thoughts and feelings to portray their relationship with 'Ed'.

We also thank the experts – doctors, researchers and expert carers – who freely share their wisdom.

*Ed says U said* taps into the evidence of experience and adapts the popular social messaging format to provide illuminating insights about an illness that, in many respects, remains a mystery.

We wish to thank everyone who has offered guidance and answered our worldwide Internet call for contributions, including: Carrie Arnold, ED Bites, www.edbites.com; Laura Collins, executive director, F.E.A.S.T. (Families Empowered and Supporting Treatment of Eating Disorders), www.feast-ed.org; Susan Ringwood, chief executive, Beat www.b-eat.co.uk; Lynn Grefe, president and chief executive officer, the National Eating

Disorders Association, USA, www.nationaleatingdisorders.org; Harriet Brown and Jane Cawley, founders, Maudsley Parents, www.maudsleyparents.org; Shannon Cutts, founder, MentorCONNECT, www.mentorconnect-ed.org; Sarah Ravin, www.drsarahravin.com; Veronica Kamerling, expert carer and trainer, Eating Disorders and Carers, www.eatingdisordersandcarers.co.uk; Daniella Allen; Jennifer Marsh; Kel O'Neill; Cathleen; Gemma; Sophie Skover, LSS Harmony, www.LSSHarmony.com; Chevese Turner, founder and chief executive officer, Binge Eating Disorder Association (BEDA), www.bedaonline.com; Gill Ryan; Pooky Knightsmith, Eating Disorders Advice, www.eatingdisordersadvice.co.uk; Kelly Richards; Anne-Sophie Reinhardt, Fighting Anorexia, http://fightinganorexia.com; Rachel McGovern; Katie Cullinane, Giant Fossilized Armadillo, www.giantfossilizedarmadillo.com; Mary Hays Brown; Avril Keanan; Michelle Preston; Suzi; Nic; Cat, Clearing Some Space, http://clearingsomespace.com; Brenda Gaddi, Digital Parents, http://digitalparents.com.au; Nicole Avery, Planning with Kids, http://planningwithkids.com; Julie Parker, Beautiful You, www.beautifulyoubyjulie.com.

Thank you to Bridget Bonnin for reading the manuscript and sharing your wisdom.

We extend appreciation to our families and friends for their encouragement, feedback and support during the creation of the concept and writing of this book, and to Editor, Lisa Clark, and her team at Jessica Kingsley Publishers for giving wings to *Ed says U said*.

# 1

## Introduction

'Understanding the voice of anorexia has felt at times like I am talking a different version of English with my daughter – when I try to provide positive feedback, it is read as failure for her or that she is fat. When she says a particular food is awful, I am constantly challenged trying to ascertain if she is giving clues as to what she actually wants me to make her eat.'

*– Mother*

'Anorexia is more than being thin – that's really the smaller part. When my sister got sick that wasn't what worried me, it was how different she was, and how she was changing mentally – the way the illness overshadowed her mind was really odd. Although I worried when she was skinny, I thought that was repairable, but mentally I sometimes thought: "Will she ever get back to herself?"'

*– Brother, a college student*

An eating disorder is a biologically based mental illness that can also cause serious physical health problems. This book seeks to explain the impact of the illness on thoughts, behaviours and relationships. The eating disorder, commonly referred to as 'Ed', is masterful at entangling not only the person who develops the illness, but also their loved ones, in its web. By understanding Ed's language, you are in prime position to encourage and facilitate recovery. Learning how to avoid the pitfalls and defuse the triggers – the words, thoughts and actions that 'feed' the eating disorder – can assist greatly in counteracting effects and fallout.

In any language, one word can have several connotations and it's the same with Ed. One word can defuse an eating disorder trigger or set it off. Unrestrained, the illness can turn a home into a minefield, with families tiptoeing around, afraid of what may come next, and beholden to Ed. Sometimes no matter what you say, the person with the eating disorder seems to take it the wrong way and pandemonium erupts.

An eating disorder, like other illnesses, has symptoms and consequences. A person sneezes and coughs because their body has a cold; a person says rude things, binges and starves because their body has an eating disorder. Heal the body, no more sneezes; heal the body, no more out-of-character behaviours, no more bingeing or starving. But an eating disorder does not make recovery easy: it affects physical, emotional and mental health, and while we all know when we have a drippy nose and cough, people with eating disorders can have great difficulty understanding the severity of their problem – in fact they may not believe they are ill at all, and be unable or helpless to acknowledge its effect on themselves or others. Even when insight is possible, and the sufferer is aware and wants to recover, the powerful hold of the eating disorder can sabotage the bravest of recovery efforts. Sufferers may function normally at some levels, but the eating disorder is a master of manipulation and misinterpretation, affecting both physical and psychological self.

*Ed says U said* provides a sneak peek into the deep, dark and often confusing world created by an eating disorder. We guide you through the layers of thought manipulation that occur as the eating disorder develops, peaks and wanes. Each conversation in this book is a real-life example where an eating disorder has influenced the dialogue. The dialogue often completely bewilders the family member, carer, friend or healthcare provider. This book also includes internal dialogues by people with experience of living with eating disorders to illustrate how decisions that appear spontaneous and impulsive are often the result of their inner anguish.

*Ed says U said* is here to help you understand how the illness influences, controls and distorts what a sufferer hears, thinks, says and does. Get ready for a chaotic ride as we take you inside the mind of people with an eating disorder (*italics* indicate the intrusive eating disorder thoughts).

You may think the language sounds like a new, not-so-nice version of *Alice's Adventures in Wonderland*; that this language is fantasy. No, the voice of eating disorders is real for those who live with it. And the good news is: full recovery *is* possible. Hold on to this knowledge like a lantern of hope as you read through the darker passages. A sense of humour and an ability to look at 'the cup half full' will be handy. Anorexia does not earn the title of having the highest death toll from any psychiatric illness lightly and, as with other eating disorders, recovery can be long and torrid. Patience is essential.

Genetics and biology play a big role in determining vulnerability for developing an eating disorder. We cannot change our genes or biology but we can learn skills and find support in our environment, to beat this illness. Persevere, for the rewards are many. *Ed says U said: Eating Disorder Translator* will help you find the way.

In *Ed says U said* we draw on our combined experience of living with eating disorders for more than 60 years. We also draw on the expert, heartfelt and candid contributions of people like us around the world who know eating disorders well: people who have lived with Ed 24/7. Researchers, medical practitioners, dieticians, psychologists and therapists can provide vital information, help and support; but voices from experience give valuable extra insight.

**Part One** sets the scene, describing who will be on stage delivering the dialogues in this book – the sufferer, carer, family members, friends, clinicians, therapists, teachers – and the invisible bad guy, 'Ed'.

**Part Two** opens with explanations of what a person living with Ed is thinking, and why, as the illness sets in. Early intervention is important for the best chance of full recovery, and you can't start too soon in building a firm foundation of knowledge on which to formulate a recovery plan.

Experienced carers – mums, dads, siblings, children, grand-parents and friends – all of whom have experience of living with Ed, offer advice in **Part Three** to help you navigate the often bewildering stage of eating disorder treatment.

In **Part Four** our survivors share their wisdom. Survivors have lived with, fought with, and banished Ed. Drawing on the clarity that recovery provides, they speak from experience on the reality of the ups, downs and everything in between that this journey entails.

Persevere, for the chapters in **Part Five** give you a glimpse through the looking glass into the hopeful future that reaching full recovery can have in store. Stories shared by eating disorder survivors show that life can be regained and dreams fulfilled. The survivors' words are a testimony of hope and encouragement to people who, through no fault or choice of their own, find themselves on an ED journey. Regaining a sense of self is possible. Regaining life, free of the eating disorder, is possible. Happiness, contentment, peace and connectedness can replace sadness, loneliness, alienation and isolation.

**Part Six** is like a cupboard stocked full of helpful resources and guidance for when an eating disorder enters your life, or the life of your loved one. Research indicates that while eating disorders affect people of all ages, they almost always start to develop or emerge in childhood or adolescence. So, from this young age, we need to be on the lookout. Prompt intervention provides best hope of a full recovery and, if you feel even a teeny bit concerned, check it out. Now.

Go to **Part Seven** to sort the facts from the fallacies about eating disorders. Misconceptions and unfounded beliefs abound and, unfortunately, they 'feed' the illness; make it worse. Myths are dangerous and deserve to be buried – without a headstone. Read Chapter 24 and explore the eating disorder advocacy and support organizations listed in the Appendix to add your beat to the drum of truth. Arming yourself with knowledge sets the scene for raising awareness and saving lives.

Above all we hope that *Ed says U said* achieves our goal of helping you understand the language and voice of eating disorders.

*June Alexander*
*www.junealexander.com*

*Cate Sangster*

# PART ONE
## Setting the Scene

# 2

## 'Ed' the Eating Disorder

'Ed' is a metaphor.

The letters ED comprise the popular acronym for 'eating disorder'. Many sufferers use the nickname 'Ed' to identify their eating disorder 'voice'. This is not an actual voice in the way we traditionally think of it. It is not a case of 'hearing voices'. Rather, it is a way of defining the negative, harsh and often destructive thoughts commonly experienced by eating disorder sufferers – and separating these thoughts from their true self.

Everyone has an internal dialogue – those conversations we have with ourselves when we are choosing which television programme to watch, deciding on the best route to work, debating where to go on holiday:

*I'd love to go to the beach – I really need a tan.*

*Hang on; your skin is way too fair for that.*

*Good point, maybe skiing then?*

*Yeah, but those winding drives up the mountain always make you car sick…*

Some people call this playing devil's advocate. Some call it the voice of reason, and others say you're debating the pros and cons. But when the thoughts no longer allow variation – when they are all about food, weight, exercise and control – and when the voice is anything but reasonable, it can become the voice of Ed.

> 'When I was little if I had a bad dream I would wake myself up and tell myself to "change the channel" on my dream. But with an eating disorder I can't change the channel. I can't think about anything else.'

Naming the eating disorder voice as Ed or anything else – some sufferers give it a female name – is a highly effective tool in identifying the destructive and negative thoughts that need to be overcome. By learning to identify and pay attention to these thoughts a sufferer can 'catch' them, recognize them, distance themselves from them and, given the skills to do so, gradually replace these thoughts with healthy and more constructive ones.

## The sufferer

The sufferer in *Ed says U said* is the person with the eating disorder. Many more inspiring and proactive words could be used – such as fighter, survivor or recovery warrior. But we choose the word 'sufferer' to convey to families, friends, teachers, coaches, healthcare providers and everyone else that, above all else, eating disorders are about suffering. An eating disorder is not something to be shrugged off. It is not a fad. It is an illness that torments the sufferer every minute of every day and night. Due to their illness, ED sufferers are often incapable of speaking for themselves: they need others to take their suffering seriously and require understanding, patience and support as they bravely set out on the path to recovery. Right from the start, Ed is a master of manipulation.

### Why I like Ed

Now we know you are wondering how anyone could possibly 'like' their eating disorder. Perhaps 'like' isn't the right word – and yet it is. An eating disorder is not a conscious choice; the illness evolves to address a perceived problem. Sure it's a temporary, dangerous and potentially fatal solution, but it seems safe from the inside. Ed gives a sense of control. It's not the type of control that goes with feeling powerful and being independent, but more a feeling (initially) of stability and security. As an eating disorder grows, it progressively consumes thoughts and numbs emotions. Unconsciously, Ed becomes a coping tool for survival – for example, in response to intense anxiety. Instead of worrying about school, peer groups, exams, puberty, sex, rape, abuse, love, life, death, anger, fear, future, past, present, thoughts become irrational; they become magnetized and fixated on routines, food and calories. Black and white. Good and bad. This feels like control. But fear is the driving force. Every moment of every day starts to revolve around it. Soon there is no room for anything or anyone else.

For a while, this approach works. For most people who develop anorexia, for instance, weight loss seems a bonus. On top of feeling better – or at least no longer feeling scared and anxious – there are the lovely comments. 'Wow, you look great!' 'What's your secret?' There might even be a little envy from peers that wasn't there before: 'I wish I had your figure.' And honestly, when nothing else is going to plan, when nothing you do feels good enough, that positive attention can replace a lonely void in your soul with an addictive warmth.

> 'My teenage daughter was happy to go out in public when very consumed by anorexia – it was like saying: "I can be so much slimmer than you can" – and when she went to hospital she worried she was not thin enough to be in the ward with the other girls.'
>
> – *Mother*

The problem is that Ed is indeed a temporary and dangerous solution. The illness develops inside the brain and, without intervention, infiltrates everywhere until scarcely any thought can pass through untouched. It dupes sufferers into thinking they are in control.

'Anything as little as eating a spinach leaf could lead me to punishing myself. Other examples are not having exercised for the day, missing a train, having an argument with a loved one or receiving anything lower than a high distinction at university; any slip up could lead me to self-harming behaviours. Many little rules ran my life.'

*— Young adult woman with self-harm behaviour*

## The carer

Depending on the age of the sufferer the carer may be a parent, sibling, grandparent, a child, partner or friends – and all of these voices appear in *Ed says U said*. A carer is not defined by who they are but by what they do. If you are prepared to step up and take responsibility 24/7 for the wellbeing of the sufferer, then you are a carer. A carer is like a recovery guide.

## The recovery path

Recovery is that part of the journey where the sufferer knows they are on the right path. Being on the recovery path does not mean a clear run to the finish line however. Slips and relapses are common and are usually the best way of learning how to better face that problem again the next time. The recovery path is a steep and winding ascent and the summit is not clearly defined – it's easy to waver, change your mind and decide the climb is too long and arduous. But stay strong in the knowledge that the view from the top is magnificent. It's worth every tear.

## Destination: recovered

Being recovered is the elusive goal. To reach the summit of the recovery journey and say 'I am recovered' is subjective – it means something different to everyone. Each sufferer has challenges and goals. For sufferers of anorexia, weight restoration is vital and yet this is only part of their recovery. Weight may not be a recovery factor for sufferers of bulimia, or binge eating disorder, but there are many other equally challenging hurdles to face. One goal, however, unites everyone: freedom. To be 'recovered' means freedom from rituals, constant and oppressive thoughts, fears, anxiety and depression. It means freedom to eat three nutritious meals and snacks daily. Importantly, with the right help, this ultimate goal of recovery from the eating disorder, and recovery of one's life, is attainable for all.

## Our story tellers

The stories you are about to read are real. They come first hand from sufferers, survivors, carers and loved ones. The stories are retold in conversation style like that found on social media – quick and direct. As with social media, our conversations have avatars – small, illustrated depictions of the speaker in each case. For clarity and simplicity, similar avatars represent people who hold similar roles – such as the various healthcare providers – and each person's role is specified with a 'handle'. A handle is a social media name which starts with the @ symbol, for example **@therapist**.

Conversation contributors align on the left side of the page, except for the sufferer and/or Ed voice – which are aligned on the right. In this way it is very easy to tell, at a glance, who is talking at any point in the conversation. So before we move on, here is a selection of the avatars you will find in *Ed says U said*:

**@mum** I don't get it! I only said it was nice to see her eat her dinner for once…

**@dad** Well it IS silly! Why doesn't she just EAT?

**@friend** Honestly, I'm so jealous. I wish I could lose weight as easily as she does!

**@sufferer** *NO ONE UNDERSTANDS!*

**@Ed** *Woo hoo – the only one she trusts is ME!*

# PART TWO
# Early Signs and Symptoms

# 3

---

# Behaviour

---

*Just because it's a problem for you, doesn't mean*
*it's a problem for me. Perhaps, when all is said*
*and done, it is you that has the problem?*

When we see someone we love acting in a strange and unexpected way, like tipping a perfectly cooked Sunday roast dinner into the bin, our first impulse is to say something like: 'What the heck are you doing?' Followed by: 'Stop it, that's a stupid thing to do.' But criticism can be the worst tack to take when the discussion involves eating disorders.

Why? Surely pointing out to your loved one how wasteful and hurtful their action is – especially when you have spent three hours preparing the ditched meal – is a reasonable response? Not when you are living with anorexia.

Perhaps this everyday example will help: imagine having a song stuck in your mind and without knowing it, you are vocalizing it. Someone asks you to please stop humming that song – does that work? Can you stop just like that? No. Perhaps you fall silent outwardly, at least, but the song stays stuck on repeat in your mind. It's still there, right? Only now you are hiding the fact you can hear it. Now imagine this repetitive thought is not a song, but an enticing 'voice' that croons day and night, helping you feel safe and less worried about things happening in the outside world. For some people, the voice is gently persistent and persuasive; it wants to be your friend, and your only friend.

The gist of its message is: 'Listen to me and do what I say; you can trust me; I will take care of you and help you solve your problems.'

Would you stop listening just because someone told you to?

By now you may already be too scared to let go of this voice, which is with you 24/7 and helps you feel safe and secure. This is what an eating disorder does. An eating disorder is like a sneaky, silent saboteur that slips in and takes over your thoughts and behaviours – so skilfully you don't even know it. This is one big reason why parents and partners trying to understand a loved one with an ED often feel they must be speaking a different language or speaking to a different person. In many ways this is what is happening. You are trying to communicate with someone who does not know they are sick, because Ed has taken over.

## Do you think I'm stupid?

 **@friend** Why do you want to feel hungry all the time? It's ridiculous not to eat!

**@teenagesufferer** *Judge me all you like babe! But I know you are saying that because you are weak and I am strong.*

*I know how confident and content I am when I'm hungry – it's the most powerful feeling!*

 **@friend** Take a proper look at yourself in the mirror – you can see you are thin.

**@adultsufferer** But truthfully – I could do with losing a bit.

**@friend** Well, you are being stupid – you're only saying that so we'll keep saying how thin you are.

**@adultsufferer** No, you don't understand, *I really do feel FAT and UGLY.*

## This is not normal

Another thing to know about eating disorder behaviour: at the same time as striving to accept that the strange behaviour of your loved one is due to their illness, remember that this behaviour isn't normal – and should not be brushed aside, dismissed, denied or laughed off. Ignoring or belittling the problem – pretending it is not there – can allow the illness to grow and really take hold, not only of the sufferer but also of you.

**@husband** Why do you do that? Why do you always take your dinner into the other room to eat it? C'mon, we want you to sit down with us and eat your dinner like a normal person.

**@wifesufferer** *eye roll* *grins* I just have to get the washing on – I'll be there in a minute.

*Yeah right, like I'm going to eat with everyone watching me.*

*It's hard enough trying to
fight the impulse to scream and spit
the food out when I'm alone.*

---

 **@parents** We are concerned about our daughter. She says she's eating, but she's looking so thin.

 **@gp** Don't worry – she isn't heading for serious trouble. It's a phase all teenagers go through on their way to being independent and responsible young adults. Whatever you do, don't pressure her at meal time – you'll only make her more determined not to eat.

**@sufferer** Dad, don't hassle me! Remember the doctor told you I am fine. AND that you aren't allowed to make me eat.

*This is so awesome! Now I
don't have to eat AND he can't hassle
me about it! *happy dance**

---

**@unistudentsufferer** I need help. I cannot stop exercising. I run until I collapse and if I eat I have to exercise again, no matter what. So half the time I just don't eat. I don't know what to do…

 **@therapist** I understand. And from what you've told me, I think it is really important that you stop running so much and eat more.

**@unistudentsufferer** *Is it really that simple? It's obvious that this is what everyone else would do – but I can't stop exercising. What if no one else feels like I do? What if I'm the only person? What if I'm just a weak freak? I must never tell anyone ever again.*

---

**@mum** His father and I are worried he's training too hard. He's getting so thin.

**@coach** He's just a wiry, trim kid. He's fine; he's clocking personal best times. You should be proud of him – he knows what it takes to be the best – and stay the best.

**@teenagesufferer** *Did you hear that! He thinks I'm the best! I can't let Coach down. I'll train harder than ever, and make sure I keep my weight down as much as possible. Any extra weight will make me a loser – and I'm a winner!*

---

**@mum** We know that she's not well, we just don't know if she's going to get better on her own or if she needs some sort of help.

**@gp** She's fine; she is nowhere thin enough for her health to be considered at risk – no eating disorder specialist would take her seriously. (And they would think you are a neurotic parent.)

**@teenagesuffererer** *I told Mum I was fat – and now the doctor has told her I'm fat too. Maybe at least this will get her off my case! I have plenty of weight left that I can lose without causing any problems. Everyone else can see how fat I am – why can't Mum?*

---

**@mum** Our daughter has an eating disorder; we are convinced of it. What can we do? How can we help her?

**@therapist1** Your daughter will benefit from participating in a behaviour course; this will fix her anxiety. You see, I believe that fixing the behaviour will fix the anxiety that in turn will fix the eating disorder.

*Several months later...*

**@mum** We enrolled for the course but halfway through we could see it was not addressing our daughter's problems. Months were passing by and she was slipping further from us. She was dying.

**@therapist2** What your daughter needs is this alternative course, on 'cool kids'. I'll arrange an enrolment straightaway.

*Later still...*

**@mum** We tried this too, but quickly realized that being 'cool' was not enough to help our daughter. We didn't know where else to turn. Our sick child was continuing to self-harm and saying she could hear voices in her head telling her not to eat.

This was not a game. This was not going to be fixed by trying to 'cheer her up' when she was literally starving to death in front of our eyes.

---

 **@parents** We have to do something. She's losing so much weight – and she's convinced she's fat, when clearly she's not. She's scaring us.

 **@gp** Don't make a big fuss over her or insist that she eat. She is an adolescent. This is what they do to exert their independence. If you pressure her to eat, you will make the situation worse. Stand back and give her space to grow up.

---

**@youngadultsufferer** Can you believe my boyfriend called me 'podgy'?

 **@mum** Well, just as well you dumped him then ☺

**@youngadultsufferer** It's got me thinking though; I might try to get fitter this holiday.

**@mum** OK – why don't you do some laps of the pool?

*Five days later…*

 **@mum** You've been in the water for ages – how many laps are you up to now?

**@youngadultsufferer** Just finished 100 laps! Can you believe it? Tomorrow I'm going to do 150. I'm aiming for 500 by the end of the week…

## I can't help it!

When an eating disorder takes hold, there's often no predicting what it will do to stay. It takes on a life of its own and is determined to get its way. Think that sounds melodramatic? Remember, the death rate for people who develop chronic anorexia, for instance, is as high as one in five (mostly heart or other organ failure, and suicide).

 **@mum** I give up – I can't say or do anything right at the moment – you're so sensitive! Why is it every time we sit down for dinner, it always ends in tears?

**@sufferer** *I don't mean to, but if I pick a fight with you and make you think it's your fault then I can pretend to be too upset to eat and you don't question that because you're so confused about what to do.*

**@dad** Stop making a scene! Everyone in the diner is looking at us! We will each eat a snack before getting back in the car to finish the drive – please, keep your voice down! You are embarrassing us!

**@sufferer** *The smell of the food is in the air – it will make calories in me if I breathe. I CAN'T stay in here. Dad is angry with me. But I can't sit still. I can't stand the pressure. He will be more than mad but I've got to run out of here. Now.*

---

 **@mum** I don't quite know how to say this, but I heard sounds of purging while you were in the bathroom; I suspect you were throwing up that beautiful pasta I made for you. At dinner you looked like you were enjoying it. What is the point of me taking two hours to cook a lovely meal that you intend to throw up? Your behaviour is disgusting and ungrateful.

**@sufferer** *I am revolting. I feel ashamed that Mum has found me out – why do I have to be such a pig? I don't mean to hurt her. Why can't I just eat a small amount and never more?*

---

 **@unitutor** You look beautiful in that dress – if I were 20 years younger I would really fall for you.

**@sufferer** *Oh no, he's hitting on me. He wants to rape me like the last man who hit on me did. Are all men like this? Do all men want to rape me? I can't think about it. I have to block it out. Concentrate on the diet. Concentrate on calories in and calories out. How much I will eat, when I will run. Get the bad thoughts out of my head.*

---

**@mum** I thought we might go shopping for some new clothes for you today.

**@sufferer** *NO! No! I can't! I can't go out of the house and have people see me and try on clothes until I hit my next weight-loss target. People will laugh at me. They will stare and the clothes won't fit and I'll have to come home with nothing, and you'll be disappointed, and…*

---

**@motherinlaw** You've got so much on your plate at the moment with the new baby, would you like me to come over and clean your house for you?

**@Ed** *She thinks you're not coping. She thinks you're too pathetic to manage. And she thinks your house is a pigsty!*

**@sufferer** *tears* Well I'm sorry my house doesn't live up to your standards of perfection! I do have a new baby, you know! I'll fix it! I just need everyone to get off my case!

## Insight

One of the scary things about an eating disorder – especially in the vital early stages – is that the sufferer almost always has no understanding that there is a problem – which is why loved ones' intervention is so important. Every now and then, a glimmer of insight shines through the wall the eating disorder is building and the truth is fleetingly illuminated – but don't be fooled into thinking this flicker of understanding will translate to action. Ed is a powerful opponent, so seek help.

> 'I suddenly noticed that I was doing the same things my mum did when I was a child: weighing myself every day, never really sitting down to eat at the table with the family, always making excuses to jump up and fetch drinks/cutlery/second helpings for everyone else and never actually getting around to eating. Perhaps my mother had an eating disorder? Perhaps I have an eating disorder? I want to be a better role model for my children.'
>
> – *Mother with anorexia*

# 4

—

# Food

—

*I love food. I just don't love eating it.*

Eating disorders are *not* 'just a diet gone too far'. An eating disorder is not a game. It is not something to be misconstrued so magazines and diet companies can increase their sales. An eating disorder is a potentially deadly illness, often accompanied by a gamut of sometimes unpredictable and prevalent food rituals and habits that make meal times a minefield.

'I'm fine. I really am. I'm just not hungry.'

Eating disorder sufferers are good at saying this – usually because it feels like reality and also to spare concern from family or friends. Sufferers often believe that they do not deserve to be fussed over. They believe their needs are less important than others and any time spent worrying about them is a waste. In this way the eating disorder keeps carers at a distance and progressively isolates the sufferer. It creates a web of secrets, lies and defensive excuses – anything to throw carers off the scent. Be aware, carers, the ED can sense when you get close to the truth and can cause a ruckus; like a bucking horse, it wants you off its back. Don't be surprised if the sufferer tries to retreat from you altogether. Hold tight, for the sufferer needs you to be strong for them.

# The secrecy

 **@mum** I don't understand why my son is losing weight. He seems to have a good appetite.

*@sufferer I save up all my calories during the day so I can use them at night when I eat the dinner that Mum cooks. I have a mental picture of what a serving of vegetables and meat looks like, and make sure I put no more than that amount on my plate – this way Mum doesn't hassle me because she thinks she's seeing me eat plenty.*

---

 **@mum** I'm worried because my daughter never eats in front of us – but in the morning when I come downstairs half the pantry has been cleaned out! It's not just that she's costing us a fortune – it's the sneaking about behind my back and lying that really annoys me.

 **@friend** Give your daughter a choice: either she stops stealing food from the pantry, or she starts paying for it out of her pocket money. Don't let her get away with it. She is plain greedy.

*@sufferer I hate myself. I don't want to binge. Every day I vow to stop. But before I know it I am bingeing again. I don't know how to stop.*

# The excuses

 **@friend** You've been on lots of diets, but you've never had rules like this before, listing what you can and can't eat. Like until now you have enjoyed eating bread. And what about red meat? Since when did that become taboo? Don't you think you're getting too carried away this time?

**@sufferer** No, I'm fine, honestly. I have designed this diet myself using the main principles from a range of diets I've read about. It's all good!

 **@friend** But there's nothing left in your diet of any nutritional substance!

**@sufferer** Nonsense – I eat plenty of fresh fruit and vegetables. I'm just really careful about not eating processed stuff and too many carbs or fat. I've cut out the foods I don't need, that's all. I'm fine. And frankly I don't think I need to defend myself to you.

---

 **@friend** I have noticed you don't bring food for yourself to our mothers' group catch-up? You just nibble on your toddler's leftovers while the rest of us are eating sandwiches and cakes.

**@sufferer** Ha! I know, but I bet I eat a bigger breakfast than you. Besides, it would be a waste to bother making two separate lunches: my daughter only eats half of what I pack anyway.

**@friend** But don't you think you should have some nourishing lunch of your own?

**@sufferer** No, I'm fine eating whatever she leaves – really ☺

*My little girl loves this playgroup but I hate people looking at what I eat. I don't think we will come again.*

## The missed opportunities

Often the signs of a budding eating disorder are obvious in hindsight. Frustratingly so. But how do you to tell the difference between a genuine, increased interest in healthy eating habits and disordered thoughts and behaviours that are precursors to an eating disorder? What happens when the signs are loud and clear but no one is listening?

**@tweensufferer** Mum, I've made a list of all the 'good' and 'bad' foods. I want to be healthy and only eat things off the 'good' foods list. I'm going to put the list on the fridge – so make sure you don't buy any more 'bad' foods, and don't let me eat any of them, OK?

**@mum** That sounds like a good plan – it's really important to eat healthily, especially at your age. Puberty can be a time when girls put on a lot of weight. I like the way you have put the calories beside each food item. That's handy for me, too.

 **@teenfriend** Why do you always eat *exactly* the same things as me?

**@sufferer** Because you are thin and I want to be thin like you ☺

 **@teenfriend** Oh you goose! I'm naturally thin – it has nothing to do with what I eat; this is just my body shape – it goes back generations.

**@sufferer** *Oh nice, so she thinks she's the only one allowed to be thin! She thinks I can't be as thin as Miss Perfect because I wasn't born that way.*

*When I'm done I'll be half her size – that'll show her.*

---

 **@gp** Your mum has noticed you are tired, you're losing weight and even though we're in midsummer, you're always rugged up as though you are cold. How's your eating?

**@teensufferer** I am very particular about what I eat. I have one cup of fortified cereal with low fat milk, half a cup low fat yogurt and a medium banana for breakfast…

**@gp** Yes, yes, well that all sounds fine. Let's move on then… I've a roomful of patients out there.

**@teensufferer** *…that's pretty much all I eat all day, but since you have not let me finish I won't be telling you – woo hoo! Go me!*

**@healthclinicnurse** When you decide to eat normally, and sustain a normal weight, everything will be fine. You'll be able to do amazing things, and have a great life, and won't feel anxious or tormented. There's really nothing wrong except you're not eating properly. You're easily fixed – eat three meals and three snacks a day. Make an appointment to see me in another six months.

**@adultsufferer** *So basically what you're saying is that I bring this on myself, that all I need to do is pull up my socks and eat normally, and my world will be perfect. I will be a six-foot Amazonian Olympic athlete with a loving husband and four kids?*

## And oh the panic

Eating disorders start out for a myriad of biological, environmental and other reasons – researchers are still working out why. Whatever the reason, the early sweetness of comforter Ed gives way to torment of monstrous and beastly proportions. Anxiety often precedes the illness and, in the case of anorexia, frequently intensifies with weight loss. Anxiety is most prevalent when eating is imminent. Behaviour can become defensive, aggressive, unpredictable and irrational. Although the reasons behind the behaviour might not be logical, the panic is real. The panic is not put on for show, attention or idle trouble making. In the mind of the eating disorder sufferer the food is poison, the enemy, the most terrifying thing ever – and the lies the Ed voice tells to stop the sufferer from eating are every bit as real.

**@tweensufferer** My bread roll is bigger than usual.

 **@mum** What do you mean? It's the same one you always have when we eat here.

**@tweensufferer** But this one is bigger!

 **@mum** It can't be – we have the same one every time – how is this one different?

**@tweensufferer** It just is. And I can't eat it! I want to go home. NOW.

---

**@teensufferer** Mum, the peas are touching the carrots! You know I can't have the coloured vegetables touching. They have to be separated by the rice otherwise they mix together and there's more calories that way. YOU KNOW THAT!

**@mum** Whatever! Serve it up yourself if you're going to be so fussy – you know all these food rules are a load of rubbish though, don't you?

**@teensufferer** *I need to count calories so that I can cope with the pressure of everything. Those peas and carrots are really bothering me.*

---

**@teensufferer** Hey Dad, I've eaten five slices of bread today. Does that seem a lot?

**@dad** Yes definitely. That is more slices than I have eaten today.

**@teensufferer** But the five slices is my total intake for the entire day.

**@dad** Well that's stupid – why did you eat all those carbs? Bread is loaded, you know. You need a variety of other foods as well.

**@teensufferer** *Oh help! What have I done! I thought plain white bread was low fat and safe because the exact number of calories in each slice is listed on the bread label. I hadn't eaten all day and was starving. How could I eat such a huge amount? I hate myself ☹ Tomorrow I'll eat nothing to compensate for being a pig today.*

---

**@mum** It's just a handful of sultanas! Why are you looking at it like that?

**@teensufferer** I can't face any more exercise today.

 **@mum** What has exercise got to do with the sultanas, for heaven's sake?

**@teensufferer** *Mum, you wouldn't understand. If I eat the sultanas I'll have to exercise to compensate for the calories... But if I don't eat them you'll be mad...*

*Please just put me out of my misery...*

---

**@teensufferer** Oh no! Don't eat that – it's got like 155 calories in it!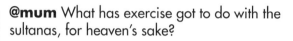

 **@friend** LOL – so what? I'm hungry and it's delicious ☺

**@teensufferer** *How can she be so carefree? Why doesn't she care? I am so terrified of eating. The guilt is too much. Why can't I eat like her?*

---

**@mum** I'm so glad you like your dinner tonight, sweetie. It's just a shame that this brand of tinned vegetables is only available from that new market out by the airport.

**@teensufferer** I don't care, Mum, this brand is the one you need to get. I like the texture of these vegetables. If you want me to eat then you'll have to get this same brand again tomorrow. I'm serious. I can't eat anything else.

**@mum** All right, don't panic, I'll go there again tomorrow. It's a 50km trip but I'll do it for you, honey.

**@teensufferer** *I feel safe eating this brand; it has the exact number of calories that I allow myself each day. I would be too terrified to eat anything else.*

---

**@mum** You are looking so worn out! Here, honey, take two of these vitamin pills every day – they'll give you an energy boost.

**@adultsufferer** Honestly, I'm fine; just need a bit more sleep.

*Do you want to make me fat? These pills have calories, and I cannot add any more calories to my day's allocation; I am fat already. Why do you want to ruin my diet?*

Or:

*There's nothing wrong with
me, I'm strong and healthy and fit,
and why would I need vitamins?*

Or:

*I don't want to feel better. I
don't deserve to feel better. Besides,
those pills are not on my list. I don't
know how many calories they contain
so to be safe I'll have none.*

Or:

*I can deal with the lethargy on
my own. Taking vitamins is cheating.*

Or:

*I don't want to put anything artificial
into my body. God knows what's really
in those pills – I don't trust them.*

# 5

## Relationships

*Too much of life is wasted running around, asking
everyone else for permission to be your own true self.*

Eating disorders love to isolate. They thrive on separating the
sufferer from their support network. The eating disorder keeps
coming up with new ploys to convince the sufferer that:

- a loved one is trying to trick and control them

- the loved one is the reason they are sick

- they are not deserving of love and assistance

- every mouthful of food is cause for guilt.

This makes for social challenges, especially around food. You've
seen it – the yelling, the slamming doors, the tears and the clingy
refusal to socialize. The situation is compounded by the sufferer's
inability to see that they are unwell. And it is worse when the family
does not understand the illness. In such circumstances, a loving
family can unintentionally 'feed' the eating disorder instead of
their child. For instance, conversations about diet don't necessarily
foster an eating disorder, but may influence a person vulnerable to
developing the illness. Of equal note, eating disorders also arise
in families where there is no parental encouragement of dieting.

**@teensufferer** Mum, I've decided I need to start eating better.

 **@mum** Sounds fair enough, honey. I'm glad you feel this way. Good nutrition is important at your age.

**@teensufferer** In fact, let's go on a diet together. It can be a mother–daughter bonding thing. We can keep each other motivated and see who can lose the most weight!

 **@mum** Hey, that sounds like fun! I can certainly do with losing a few kilograms. And we can go walking together in the mornings before school and help each other out with diet recipes and tips.

**@teensufferer** Awesome! Let's go to the bathroom right now and do our first weigh in!

---

**@teensufferer** Do you think I look fat?

 **@dad** No, no, you just need to tone up a bit. I can see you haven't been doing much exercise lately!

**@teensufferer** *What? But I've lost weight and have been doing circuits every day! I must look huge! I'm Dad's princess and I'm not measuring up. Tomorrow I will halve the calories and double my exercise routine.*

## Family ties

 **@mum** When we get to your aunt's house, please don't make a fuss about the food she serves for lunch. Just eat it. Think about others for once, and let's have a nice, pleasant family outing.

**@teensufferer** *Sure, keep the family freak under wraps. Don't talk; don't tell. Never let on that we might all not be quite so perfect. Far better to keep up appearances than to let others know my shameful little secret. Sure, I'll pretend to be perfect. I'll hide the food in my pocket when Aunt is not looking or feed it to her favourite pot plants.*

---

 **@sister** You're doing it again! You're ruining everyone's fun with your stupid rules. Can't do this, can't do that. Can't eat here, can't miss your run. Blah blah blah. Just lighten up and think about the rest of us for a change.

**@sufferer** These rules are important, all right, so leave me alone!

*If only she knew how much I did think about everyone else! I feel guilty – I know I'm ruining everyone else's fun. But if I don't*

*stick to my routine... I can't even bear to*
*think about it. I have to. I have to. I have to.*
*I need the rules to get through each day.*

---

 **@nana** Why don't you put sugar in your tea any more?

**@sufferer** I'm trying to be healthy, Nana.

 **@nana** You don't need to diet, you've filled out nicely since I last saw you. And besides, you must know that boys like girls with curves.

**@Ed** *Oh my gosh! She just called you fat!*

**@sufferer** Listen, it's my body and I'll do what I want. There is no way I'm adding extra calories to my food just so I can be a 'good catch'. We don't all want to be married at 18 you know.

---

 **@dad** Why don't you return your mother's phone calls? It's rude not to do so.

And as for cancelling your trip home this Christmas – unforgivable!

**@youngadultsufferer** Sorry.

*Oh thank goodness – now they are mad with me I have an excuse not to face them. No questions about my weight. No having to avoid eating food prepared by other people. No having to interact. I can stay in my dorm by myself. It is so much better this way.*

## Adult relationships

The line between adult partnership and an increasing concern for a partner's mental and physical health can become blurred when an eating disorder develops. Filling the role of both partner and carer is challenging.

 **@husband** You say you love me, but you behave like you can't stand me. You won't even let me hug you! What did I do wrong?

**@sufferer** Oh nothing, honey, I've a stomach ache at the moment.

*I want so much to let him hold me – but I can't stand the feeling of shame when he touches my fat. I'm so disgusting – if he feels how revolting I am, he will be repulsed too.*

---

 **@boyfriend** My sister had anorexia, and I can see signs of the symptoms developing in you. I want you to seek help.

**@sufferer** Thanks for your concern but I'm fine. I've just been under a bit of stress lately – too much studying, you know.

*Oh perfect, so now he thinks I'm as dippy as his sister?*

*I'm a med student, for crying out loud! Eating disorders are reserved for silly girlie girls who spend all day looking in the mirror – not me! How much do I have to do to be good enough for him?*

---

 **@boyfriend** Is that all you're going to eat?

**@sufferer** Are you serious? Who do you think you are? My mother?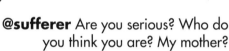

 **@boyfriend** No, I just meant that I'm worried about you – you're looking really thin and you eat no more than a sparrow.

**@sufferer** Well at least I'm not one of those girls who let themselves go when they get a boyfriend – I'm making sure I stay fit and healthy, and look nice for you, that's all.

*I feel more confident and sexier when I don't eat. I like it when he feels my bones. But I'm terrified there is still some fat and he will find it.*

---

**@sufferer** *I need to tell my partner what's really going on.*

**@Ed** *No way, he'd be so embarrassed if he knows you're feeling this way. You must think about his job and his standing in the community – if word gets out that you have an eating disorder you will ruin everything for him.*

**@sufferer** *But I need emotional support from him.*

**@Ed** *But this is a girlie problem; he will think you're weak and he doesn't understand or have time for these sorts of things. Seriously, he will laugh and not want to talk about it – you'll make him uncomfortable and he'll think you're a liability. And he'll divorce you.*

---

**@husband** You're not going out running again! This is the third time today – you keep leaving me with the kids for an hour at a time – it's not fair – I've got things to do too.

**@sufferer** Like what? You just want to watch the TV, but I have an important schedule and sticking to it is vital. I need to train, to maintain my fitness.

**@husband** Train for what?

**@sufferer** Well, nothing specific. I just need to. Stop making this harder for me.

 **@husband** Making what harder?

**@sufferer** Nothing, please stop badgering me – I have to go now before it gets dark.

 **@husband** *sigh*

---

**@sufferer** Have I eaten enough, is that amount OK?

 **@boyfriend** Yeah, if that's all you want.

**@sufferer** *I think something's wrong with me. Half a potato, half a carrot and ten peas, no meat or bread – I used to eat a lot more than this. Why can't he see it? I wish he could be stronger for me. Does he just not care? Maybe I'm just imagining that I have a problem? Tomorrow, nine peas...*

## Between friends

**@mum** Why don't you want to go on your club's hockey interstate tour?

**@teensufferer** I don't know. I don't like to be away from home.

**@mum** But you love all your hockey friends and you are one of the team's best players. You will be letting the side down.

**@teensufferer** I know, it's just such a big group of girls, and I don't like all that noise. And nothing will be the same as it is at home. It won't be my bed, or my pillow and covers. And it won't be warm, and the food won't be nice like you cook it. I just don't want to go.

*My food and exercise routines take up a lot of time and I can't risk upsetting them. I don't want my friends to know about them because they might laugh at me and tease me.*

**@friend** We're all going out to dinner on Friday – want to come?

**@youngadultsufferer** Oh I wish I could, but I already have plans…

*I can't go! When there's noise around me at dinner it's like I'm in a glass bubble. I can't hear the conversation. All of my friends will be laughing and I won't know what about because I won't be able to think about anything but the food. I'm better off at home alone.*

---

**@teensufferer** I don't want to go to her party, Mum.

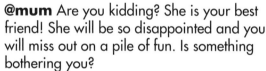

 **@mum** Are you kidding? She is your best friend! She will be so disappointed and you will miss out on a pile of fun. Is something bothering you?

**@teensufferer** Please Mum; I just want to stay home with you. We can do something special together. I know, we can cook Dad a surprise dinner! We can cook roast beef AND potatoes. And for dessert I can make that double chocolate cake he likes so much. C'mon Mum, this will be much more fun!

*Everyone will be eating food
and laughing at the party – I don't
know how they do it without feeling
guilty – I feel I don't belong.*

## Working relationships

 **@workcolleague1** She's looking so thin. She's not healthy – I can see in her eyes how unhappy she is. Do you think we should tell her we are worried about her and ask if something is troubling her?

 **@workcolleague2** As long as she keeps doing her job competently, I don't think it's any of our business. Everyone's entitled to a midlife crisis ☺

**@sufferer** *I wish my colleagues had
asked: 'Are you OK?' A small part of me
knows I'm in dire need of help but I don't
know how to ask for it.*

Or:

*I can't afford to lose my job. I
must not take any more sickies. I'm
terrified my superiors will ask questions,
discover my eating disorder secret, tell
me I'm obviously not fit to do my job
and send me to Social Security...*

# 6

## Sense of Self

*People always say: 'Just be yourself.' I don't
have a clue what they are talking about.*

Before a person develops an eating disorder, their thoughts comprise one main 'voice'. Thought conversations on what to say, what to wear, who to see and what to eat take the form of 'What do I want to do?' Decision-making seems pretty straightforward and uncomplicated. But when an eating disorder develops, the conversation becomes busier, louder and more chaotic, with conflicting thoughts and 'voices'. The Ed interloper doesn't care what you want. It wants to control, isolate and destroy. It yells in your mind 24/7 and you have great difficulty distinguishing 'normal' thoughts from the Ed thoughts. The more Ed takes hold, the more it suppresses the real you. As the sense of self erodes, external measures, such as weight loss successes, are clung to for validation of worth and appeasement of anxiety.

People who have experienced an eating disorder explain:

'At first I knew why I was doing it – I wanted to lose a bit of weight to be fitter. But somewhere along the line it spun out of control. I was no longer an athlete – I was an eating disorder. I no longer worried about my track times; all I thought about when I ran was how many calories I was burning. It was no longer me inside my own body.'

'The anorexia helped me to control how I felt, and numb any sense of sadness and anger. It enabled me to control at least what I thought was myself, because I understood I could not control the outside circumstances. But the more I controlled what I ate and lost weight, the harder it became to see anything rationally.'

'Nobody understood why I was worried about losing weight – everyone thought it was great and told me so. They also said I should be grateful for being able to lose weight so easily.'

'I was a tubby ten-year-old and my mother said: "If you want to lose weight, exercise more and eat right." So I started to lose weight and was getting compliments like: "Hey, you have lost a lot of weight" and "You look great." It really gave my confidence a boost. So I thought, "If I lose more weight I will look even better and feel even more confident."'

'I would say to myself things like "Once I lose enough weight then I will be cool enough to wear any sort of clothes I like" and "Once I lose enough weight everyone will like me" – but no matter how much weight I lost I was still just me.'

'I kept telling myself that if I lost more weight, everything would be all right and then I would be able to eat. But it was never all right. No matter how much weight I lost it was never enough.'

'I wanted help, but felt too fat to be believed. My biggest fear was that my doctor wouldn't be able to hide a little smirk and eye-roll if I said: "I think I might have an eating disorder." I was sure she would think I was behaving like a hypochondriac.'

'One guy said he liked me, and later raped me. I felt ashamed, dirty and stupid and guilty for getting into that situation. In hindsight, I think I wanted to be rid of my old self and started receding into and shrinking myself, and imposed very strong and strict discipline on my eating and exercise. My little diet soon became a more punishing regime. When I returned to university I started running every morning and evening, hardly eating or going out, and focused on my work.'

'I used the calorie counting as a substitute for dealing with depression. It was a distraction for a time – and although it worked well at keeping the depression hidden, it took a toll on my body and mind as I lost more and more weight.'

'My inner chaos accelerated: arrested twice for drinking, losing my football coach and mentor in a car accident, abusing alcohol, not eating, cheating on my girlfriend, dating two girls at once, and failing on the playing field. Yet nobody saw my life in a bad light. Guys thought I was cool, girls still thought I was a sweetheart, and my parents thought I was a wonderful son. Anorexia was settling in and I had no idea who I was.'

'After losing a little weight, I did not feel good admitting this to myself, but it calmed my anxiety. This is what anorexia does.'

'I stopped socializing almost completely. I lived in an on-campus suite with three other girls (close friends since freshman year), and kept to myself more and more, refusing to attend meals with them and hardly ever going out on weekends. I became increasingly worried about schoolwork, constantly doing assignments and reading chapters, even if they weren't due for many weeks. I also exercised rigidly, and became anxious if I didn't exercise a certain amount every single day.'

'I began to realize I was quite good at this losing weight thing and initially enjoyed the buzz and positive attention it gave me.'

'I was sure my friends, who expressed concern about my weight loss, were really jealous of my willpower and control, because I was able to succeed where they had failed. I was determined to show them I could do even better and lose more weight. It soon got to the stage where I could not eat even if I wanted to. I would be overcome with fear and guilt.'

'After the birth of my baby I told a fit friend of mine what my goal weight was and she just laughed because that was thinner than she was and she didn't believe I could do it. I felt that she thought she was better than me. So I showed her.'

'A friend of mine had a baby at the same time as me. She is tall and beautiful and has an accent so always catches people's attention when we go out. To top it off her house always looks fantastic. But I knew she would have more trouble than me getting the weight back off. I remember thinking "At least I can do one thing right."'

'I loved comments like "I'm worried about you, you're too thin." To me this meant, "I'm so envious of your ability to succeed – what's your secret?"'

'All my friends were thin and I felt like I would be "letting the group down" if I weren't thin as well. I felt an enormous pressure to stay thin, as I thought they would be disappointed if I ruined our group's "look". I didn't want to be the fat chick in the group. But soon I found I could not eat even when I wanted to do so.'

'I had been underweight in my teens and early twenties and as far as I can remember it didn't take an enormous toll on my health or emotional stability then – so why should it now? I didn't take into account that I was 20 years older and post-natal, and that quite frankly all this dieting was taking a cumulative and terrible toll on my body.'

'Our family has many secrets in the name of keeping up appearances. So many, I forget who I'm supposed to be at any one time. Don't tell your grandmother "this"; don't tell your father "that". Tell people you want to be "this" when you grow up. It's so stressful; I can't keep all the stories straight. Concentrating on my food intake and exercise feels like the only thing I can keep under any control – and get right.'

# Survivor story: we think you have an eating disorder

Kelly is a wife, mother and postgraduate psychology student in Melbourne, Australia. She has a part-time job on a university health research project and is a volunteer in the area of palliative care.

Although she will never be grateful for having anorexia, Kelly is thankful for the intense gratitude she now experiences in being healthy and happy. Kelly describes how she began her recovery journey:

## *Diagnosis*

My parents planned their approach under the guise of a family dinner. Dad said casually: 'Excuse me, Kelly – can you come in here for a bit?' The terribly awkward conversation was filled with lots of serious faces (our family didn't do formal chats), long silent pauses, rehearsed words. There was no time for my usual *'I'm OK – over 18 – worry about someone with real problems'* spiel.

'Kelly, we think you have an eating disorder,' Mum said hastily, using her whole body to get the words out.

I had had hundreds of conversations with my parents about my weight and my diet – usually rushed and ending with someone (usually me) slamming something or yelling about 'getting off my back' and 'making a big deal out of nothing'. So far, that retaliatory response had worked.

But this time my parents' approach felt more like an unprovoked assault; like someone had confronted me on the street and punched me full-blown in my chest. Because really what my parents were saying was: 'Love, we had great hopes for you but unfortunately you have turned out a failure.' Cornered, I did what was needed to appease them and promised to make an appointment with an eating disorder professional.

So here I was sitting in the slick polished waiting room, late on a Wednesday afternoon after managing to leave work early, with one of my black shiny stiletto heels tapping on the polished timber floor way too frantically. I had expected to trot off to some sort of medical clinic where skeleton type figures would be waiting to be weighed; instead here I was, in the waiting room of some slick city psychologist. (Little did I know, this was just the start of a lifetime of changes.)

I wanted the psychologist to understand right from the start that I wasn't supposed to be sitting here, that despite a few eating issues and a set of worried parents, I was someone in control and, for the most part, together: I had a job, friends and a house, got out regularly, socialized and exercised. She would realize soon enough that I was wasting her time.

'So – what brings you here today?' the psychologist said.

'Um, you see, I do eat; it's just that I'm something of a vegetarian. I get busy and don't always have time to eat.'

On and on, it went like that; bits of information blurted out…

*You've made a mistake!*

Voices screamed in my head but it was already too late. Besides, I knew in the deepest part of my soul that I wasn't living the life that I was meant to be living. I just didn't know how to live another way. I might have denied it then but the push from my parents to enquire about an ED had been an answer to my silent call for help.

That first therapist appointment became a blur. 'Maybe I'm in shock,' I thought, trying to remember what had been said about doctors' consultations, food diaries, gaining weight, *weekly* counselling appointments, accepting support, possible depression. I mean, I didn't even know I was sick. I felt an urge to apologize for wasting her time and explain that my eating issues weren't really that *bad*.

## Doctor appointment

**Doctor:** You *just* make the healthy weight range for your height…

*Are you serious? Do you know what that means!?*

**Doctor:** …but this chart is very wide ranging, so it doesn't mean that you don't have any adverse health effects that accompany eating disorders…

*I don't care how wide ranging that stupid chart is – I prefer not to be on it, and want to beat my fists on the desk to override the flush of shame.*

*I was getting all carried away with that psycho-mumbo-jumbo – thinking that I had an eating disorder – as if something like that could happen to me – but now I'm told I'm not thin enough and I have the evidence to prove it!*

**Doctor:** We need all your test results before we can make conclusive assessments about negative impacts on your health, but you might be one of the lucky ones.

*'Lucky?' Just when I have been thinking that perhaps, it might be possible, that I have an eating disorder; that there might actually be something wrong with me, beyond needing to 'get over myself'; the doctor pulls the rug from under my feet.*

**Doctor:** Do you throw up?

**Kelly:** No I don't.

I say this a little too quickly, shaking my head indignantly. The doctor speaks in a matter of fact way, like she asks people these questions every day; I feel like she has thrown iced water on my face.

*It's enough to have the allegation of one eating disorder label hanging over my head let alone another.*

**Doctor:** Do you use dietetics, diet pills or laxatives?

**Kelly:** Um…well I have taken laxatives a few times, but not *recently* and not to lose weight – just to help when my system gets a little – sluggish.

*I hope that word is good enough to fool her.*

*My face flushes hot pink. The pain, the cramps, have been excruciating; bathroom memories bombard my mind.*

The doctor is working through what seems a patient symptom list.

**Doctor:** Do you eat meat?

**Kelly:** Meat? Not really…yes to chicken and fish.

I speak quickly, hoping to divert this line of questioning by explaining I have been a 'vegetarian' for many years (even though not based on legitimate political, philosophical or dietary grounds).

*I didn't know much about eating disorders. The only person I knew who had an eating disorder was my flat mate. She was five years older than me; very attractive – a real head turner. She wrote a letter once and left it on my pillow – she suspected that I had anorexia and expressed concern. I laughed and threw her letter in the bin, questioning if our friendship had run its course. I was 24.*

**Doctor:** Do you menstruate regularly – when was your last pap smear – are you on the Pill?

*My reproductive organs twist and hold together with the mere inference to the word p.e.r.i.o.d let alone s.e.x.x.x.*

*I want out of the room. I have officially had enough.*

*What I really need is to go for a run, so I hope I'm home before dark.*

**Kelly:** I've experienced irregular periods over the years but my cycle is now normal, which means I have gained enough weight to be considered 'healthy'; and I am not on the Pill, mainly because I am not dating anyone and haven't in a while.

*There is also my fear of gaining unnecessary weight, but I'm not about to incriminate myself further.*

**Doctor:** Depression, anxiety?

*Is sculling a bottle of vodka or taking a handful of sleeping tablets to get through the bouts of crying unusual? Only last Saturday morning, while hanging clothes in the courtyard, the sun shining, I was struck with a force like a baseball bat to the knees – overwhelmed with intense feelings of loneliness and loss, I cried non-stop for the rest of the day.*

**Doctor:** At work, do you eat in or take-away?

**Kelly:** Take-away.

*I really feel the need to say, scream actually, that I don't want any lunch at all. My choice is to sit at my desk eating two pieces of fruit every day. This way I avoid feeling unbearably FULL and physically sick and don't have to bear witness to clusters of people in the dining hall, chatting and laughing as a reminder of something that I never do.*

## Telling people

My immediate family had already been told of my diagnosis. One call to my mother and the word was out. Every family member began telephoning with invitations to dinners or random chats that started with 'Just rang to see how you are going.'

**Mother:** Would you like to come around for dinner – I can make whatever you like.

**Brother:** We are going out Saturday night – it will be fun! Please come.

**Sister:** Oh, and what about Sunday – we'll come around for lunch or we could always do brunch?

*All I want is to be left alone.*

Dad was the only family member who didn't take my news well.

**Dad:** You are wallowing in self-pity. You need to get on with it, that's all. You don't need to pay top-dollar to some fancy specialist in the city to tell you what to do. You just need to EAT – how hard can that be…what sort of qualifications does that doctor have anyway?

I sit silent, stunned, feeling 16, waiting for him to get to the inevitable part about being grateful for the food I had, when people in Ethiopia are starving, dying. But he goes for a more sensitive hit.

**Dad:** If you would just meet a nice man, things will probably change overnight!

*I feel my father has kicked me while I'm already slumped in the gutter.*

## Friends

With family fully briefed, it's time to tell my friends. Not my idea but another promise made to the psychologist. Apparently it is necessary to 'out' myself from the eating disorder closet.

Avoiding calls from friends is no longer an option.

**Kelly:** Would you believe I'm seeing a 'specialist' and receiving treatment for an eating disorder?! I just need to eat a little more…I'll be better in no time.

**Friend, M:** I always knew.

'M' and I had lived together the year before and I had hated her interrogations. She had questioned my diet many times and sensed my unhappiness. We had been friends since high school and she now worked in London as a nanny. She was a year older – popular, attractive and social. Often I had wondered about our fundamental differences. Now, tears catch me by surprise. Something about the way 'M' speaks, her empathy and concern, makes me feel quite tragic.

**Friend, L:** How long will recovery take?

'L' is three years older, an inspiring interior designer with a long-term partner and baby on the way. We have spent a lot of time together. 'L' is genuinely concerned.

**Friend, P:** You look fit and healthy to me. Are you sure they have it right? I guess you have always been fussy with food choices – though I thought you were simply watching your weight.

'P' is a schoolteacher and we have often competed in fun-runs and bike rides together.

**Cousin, D:** No way! You? No. Can't be right. You are the one always solving everyone else's problems!

'D', divorced, with three young children, is a decade older than me. We caught up for coffee regularly, played competition tennis and went to movies together.

*She's right; I was the person always dishing out advice, counselling those 'in need'.*

**Cousin, D:** No offence, but don't you have to be really thin, to be anorexic?

*My stomach is in knots.*

## Frequent question: What do I say when someone tells me they have an eating disorder?

 **@survivor** Everyone is different and everyone needs different things from their support people. But if a loved one or friend has confided in you it is because they want you to be part of their support network – so keep this fact in mind when responding. Brushing off their concerns because you are scared or want to appear confident will come across as not caring. Listen. Ask questions. Admit you don't know the answers. Share your concerns. And above all let them know you love them and will not abandon them.

### Unhelpful responses

Sufferers share responses we do not want to hear again:

'The doctor told me today I have an eating disorder…'

- No way!

- Yeah, I think I had that once.

- Ha! I wish I had your problem! Have you seen how much weight I've put on lately?

- No! You're just fit and healthy.

- Don't be silly, you just need to eat properly.

- Don't worry, you'll be better in no time.

- You just need to find yourself a good man, and then you won't have time for all this.

- No, that can't be right, you don't have any problems! You're the one who's always fixing our problems.

- No, you're not thin enough to have anorexia.

- Aren't you too old to have an eating disorder?

- Not you too! Does everyone have an eating disorder these days?

- But you look so amazing!

- Ooh, can I catch a bit of that from you? I do so want to fit into this dress!

- I always knew there was something wrong with you.

- For God's sake don't tell anyone!

## Helpful responses

Responses that will help promote trust with the sufferer include the following:

- Wow, that sounds really serious! How do you feel about that?

- You know, I feel very relieved. I have been feeling concerned about you for some time. You have been really brave, going to the doctor and telling him how you feel. How can I help? I'll be your friend through all this.

- I was diagnosed with anorexia as a teenager – I know I've never told you that, but I want you to know you are not alone. What can I do to support you?

- I have thought this for a while, but didn't know how to raise it with you. I'm so glad that you have realized it for yourself and I will stand by you.

- I'm so sorry you're not well. I am here for you. Do you have professional help in place or can I help you organize that?

- Let me know what is helpful – and also what is not helpful for you through all of this.

- I know you can get through this – but you will need lots of support. I am ready to give you this, even when you don't think you want it. Because I love you.

- Thank you for trusting me enough to share this with me. You have nothing to be ashamed of, but I will not break this trust you have in me.

- Recovery is possible.

If you find yourself speechless, the physical contact of a hug can speak louder than words.

# PART THREE
Treatment

# 7

## Look Out for the Triggers

Gaining a life back from the grip of Ed is not an easy ride but hold on – this section is for you. The transition into the treatment stage, where Ed is challenged, often results in unexpected consequences. Our search for dialogue for *Ed says U said* uncovered many misinterpretations that ignite distress and concern but two stand out. One such dialogue time bomb causes agony and setback for people recovering from an eating disorder. The other 'bomb' is a question that people in recovery like to ask, and which carers, family and friends identify as being particularly treacherous to answer. Being prepared will put you one step ahead.

## Most loaded comment

'You look great!'

 **@survivor** Danger. Danger. Danger!

Why? you ask. Surely encouraging and complimenting your loved one

when they really do look so much
better is the best thing you can do?

'You look great' focuses on the sufferer's
physical appearance and this is usually
the source of their most intense distress.
Your intentions may be heartfelt, but in the
mind of your loved one you are drawing
attention to the fact they have gained
weight. Even if you don't think you are
doing this, Ed does, and creates a ruckus.

'Ed' interpretations include:

**@Ed** *She means I am 'fat', of course.*

Or:

*See, I am so fat everyone can see it.*

Or:

*They are gloating because I am
as fat as them now; there's nothing
special about me any more.*

Or:

*If I look so great at this weight
why do I have to keep adding more?
It's all a trick to make me fatter.*

Or:

*Well, now I know what a liar she is
because clearly I do not look great. I am
enormous and she is trying to deny it.*

Solution: avoid making comments that refer to physical appearance.
Ask about a latest book release, movie or a favourite sport.

## Most loaded question

'Have I gained weight?'

 **@experiencedcarer** This question is tricky to answer tactfully any time, and more so when an ED is involved. Avoid distress by being prepared and delivering a confident, non-negotiable answer.

Solution: build on these suggested responses:

- We have discussed this before and agreed that only your eating disorder specialist will answer this question.

- I will not answer this question, but would like you to think about how you will feel if you have lost weight? And how you will feel if you've gained weight?

- This is not a question I will answer but I am happy to discuss why you think you need to know.

- You know perfectly well that I will not answer this question no matter what your weight, so there's no point in making assumptions from my refusal to respond.

- Your eating disorder wants to know the answer to that question, not you. I will not talk to your eating disorder.

## Carers

Eating disorders are complicated and treatment for recovery takes a long time – we hope that it is only months but it often takes years. Parents or other prime loved ones who accept the role of carer are integral to recovery. A visit to the family doctor is generally the first of many steps. If your loved one gets a correct diagnosis the first time you seek help, you are doing well. You are on first base. Even so, your loved one is unlikely to be 'fixed' by next Christmas. Prepare yourself for a long haul. Arm yourself with knowledge about eating disorders and evidence-based treatment options. Like going into battle, prior preparation and planning are important. Seeking treatment early, when symptoms are first suspected or noticed, gives the best chance of resuming a normal lifestyle as soon as possible. Oh, and remember that the eating disorder will attempt to throw you off the trail. Stick with it.

## Children and adolescents

Early intervention with Maudsley Family Based Treatment (FBT) is currently the best, front-line evidence-based treatment for anorexia nervosa in children and adolescents. If the family doctor has limited experience of eating disorders and has not heard of this treatment, describe the signs and symptoms evident in your child and, if need be, request a referral to an ED specialist. You may wonder where your lovely child has vanished to – well, they are still there, and yes, they can come back – it is just that for now their true self is hidden under the bossy and manipulative illness. Your love, understanding and support can help to defuse the illness triggers and behaviours. Try to maintain calm. Getting frustrated with the treatment process or the person will hamper recovery. On the other hand, joining support groups and learning coping skills will help both you and your loved one get through this nightmarish time as quickly as possible.

## Adults

If you are an adult seeking help for the first time, it is likely you have been suffering for some years already. Be brave, make an appointment with your GP and describe your symptoms thoroughly. Many sufferers have common experiences so don't hold back in describing your fears and behaviours in relation to food – and be prepared to seek a referral to an ED specialist. Going home with a prescription for medication to treat anxiety or depression won't be enough to do the trick. Eating disorders are often associated with anxiety and depression but require special treatment. They are not like an infection that can be treated with a course of antibiotics. They involve many thought and behavioural processes which must be 'rewired, redirected and restructured' through refeeding, skills training and therapy. Evidence-based treatment providers consider refeeding the essential first step in treating anorexia nervosa. Food becomes the primary medicine, both for the body and the brain. In hospital or residential settings, patients unable to cooperate with refeeding efforts may be prescribed nasogastric or intravenous feeding. At home, the recovery guide – usually parents or partners – supervises eating until full weight restoration is achieved. It is helpful to remember that, just like you would not choose to have cancer, nobody chooses to have an ED. You are not weak. You need and deserve help. With guidance from therapists and support of loved ones, you can recover – at any age.

## Frequent question: Why is this taking so long?

### Unhelpful responses

Unhelpful things people say to the sufferer:

- I thought you would be over it by now.

- Aren't you trying?

- Have you checked the doctor's qualifications?

- That doctor is just trying to get more money out of you.

- I think you need to up your medication.

Unhelpful things people say to the carer:

- Why aren't you back at work? You can't just keep taking time off. It's not like your daughter is a baby!

- Just tell her to pull her socks up and stop wasting her life.

- Your son needs a good kick in the pants. That will give him something else to think about.

- The longer you keep indulging her, the longer she is going to keep taking advantage of you.

- She just needs to come and stay with me for a while – I'll fatten her up.

## Experience stories: guilt and shame

*Having a mental illness can feel a bit like having leprosy.*
*People feel sorry for you and afraid of you at the same time.*

Guilt and shame go hand-in-hand with eating disorders. The secrecy of the behaviours and the perpetuation of media sensationalism affect carers and sufferers alike. But perhaps most difficult are comments from people we trust – including friends, family and medical professionals. The following comments are here to educate rather than to condemn:

 **@adult** Just eat, will you.

**@Ed** *You are so pathetic.* *Stop making such a fuss.*

 **@survivor** Many people said this to me while I was sick. And I know it makes sense and the illness makes no sense – but this comment does not help. It makes you feel more useless, more helpless, more pathetic, and more out of control.

**@familyGP** Don't worry, he can't possibly have an eating disorder, he's a boy!

 **@survivor** Although the statistics show that more females have eating disorders than males, the incidence of males diagnosed is growing. Yes, men (and boys) get eating disorders too.

---

 **@gp** You're choosing not to eat, you selfish girl. You are tearing your family apart, your parents will divorce, your sister is depressed and you are causing the family finances to dry up.

**@Ed** *You are doing this on purpose because you are an attention seeker.*

 **@survivor** He really laid on the guilt trip and I took it all to heart. I knew I was shallow and ugly inside and out. I was screwing around a lot of people's lives and was helpless to do anything about it. Hatred is too weak a word to describe how I felt about myself.

---

 **@ERdoctor** Just eat this custard tart will you? My two-year-old grandson would wolf it down in no time. Can't you see you are worrying your parents with this more than childish behaviour?

**@Ed** *He thinks you are so immature. No one likes you – you are such a wimp. You'd be better off dead.*

 **@survivor** All I could think was I hate you, you stupid man. Stop making me feel guilty. I already feel bad enough.

---

 **@seniorEDclinician** Do you know what you've got? You've got anorexia. Let me give you the facts: a third of people with this get better, a third have it for the rest of their lives and a third die. It's up to you which third you want to end up in.

**@Ed** *Give up now. It's hopeless – you're going to die. There's no way out, so you'll be in the third that die.*

 **@survivor** I was 13, it was my first hospital admission and I was hooked up to all these tubes and a heart monitor. I had no idea what was going on and I was terrified. All I heard was I was going to die because I could not see any way of stopping it.

---

**@adultsufferer** There is something else I wanted to ask about... I was diagnosed with anorexia a few months ago and want to talk to you about what I can do to overcome and prevent potential impacts on my ability to get pregnant.

**@obstetrician** OK, let's see here. Hop on the scales. Oh, you're not that underweight, I weighed only a few pounds more than that at your age. Eat some of those yummy rich foods that I'm not allowed to eat any more at my age (ha ha) to gain a few pounds, and you'll be fine.

**@Ed** *I can't believe you even bothered mentioning that – you make such a big deal about everything. No one wants to hear your 'woe is me' story.*

**@survivor** I thought I was being really brave disclosing my anorexia diagnosis to the obstetrician but she brushed it off as though it wasn't important. She made me feel as though I was making too much fuss about it. She made me feel embarrassed and I made a mental note not to mention the illness again.

**@familyfriend** Give her to me for a month and she'll be fine.

**@experiencedcarer** My first interpretation of this comment was that I was doing a bad job and anyone could do better than me. But the therapist helped me see that in reality it was just that my friend didn't understand the illness.

**@experiencedcarer** People assume we aren't trying hard enough to find a 'cure' for our daughter and insist on giving advice on all things we 'should' be trying, including hypnosis, crystals, faith healers and herbalists. All such remedies are most likely to be fantastic in certain situations but not when your daughter is dying.

---

 **@experiencedcarer** The doctors at the hospital saved her life but didn't treat her illness. We were not included in the treatment plan and could visit only one hour a day. The implication was: leave her with us and we will fix (fatten) her up – you are of no further use. You can guess what happened when she came home. Yes, she lost weight. To beat Ed, we needed an integrated approach.

---

 **@therapist** Your hovering over her every meal is keeping her sick. She won't truly get better until you cut the apron strings and make her learn some independence.

 **@experiencedcarer** The therapist believed I was the cause of my daughter taking so long to recover – what she didn't know was the few times we had tried to reduce our constant support, our daughter had relapsed severely. She still had no drive to nourish herself – we weren't feeding her to control her, we were feeding her to keep her alive.

---

**@psychiatrist** She has a serious personality disorder resulting in her inability to make decisions.

 **@experiencedcarer** He talked as though he knew her, but in reality he had interviewed my daughter for only 20 minutes before making this diagnosis. My daughter had no ability in making wise decisions in any aspect of her life due to the effects of malnourishment. This needed attending to first.

---

 **@experiencedcarer** Our daughter refused to go to the psychiatrist again and this time we didn't try to overrule her. The first time we went, he kept looking at his watch, and that stressed our daughter out, too. She felt unimportant and that she was not being listened to.

---

 **@psychiatrist** Sorry I'm a bit late for our first appointment. I've had new office furniture delivered to my consulting suite today. It's half set up and looking good! I'll finish unpacking the books straight after this appointment. The sofa is so comfortable I might sleep here tonight!

 **@survivor** I was so embarrassed. I felt like I was taking this psychiatrist away from something he would much rather be doing. Clearly his new furniture was more important than me and I was wasting his time.

---

**@gp** I'm sorry I kept you waiting but it took me over an hour to convince the young girl before you that she needed to eat. She was having a really serious crisis – I knew you would understand and not mind waiting.

**@survivor** I did understand that this girl needed my GP's help, but the GP's comment made me feel I was way down on her priority list because I was a middle-aged woman and that being an adult, I should be coping better than I was. I felt like the GP was saying: 'This young girl really needs me – you don't.' And that hurt.

---

**@medicalstudent** Do you realize you will look much prettier if you put on a few kilograms?

*@Ed See, I told you you were ugly. There, even he thinks you're an ugly fat cow.*

**@experiencedcarer** I could physically see my poor little daughter get smaller as the medical student said this. The words came out of his mouth with no understanding of the consequences – he really thought that pointing out how awful she looked would motivate her! But it made her feel worse.

# 8

## Behaviour

*If I behave the way you expect me to, does*
*that mean I'm doing it right?*

Recovery seems endless due to the challenging behaviours that
are symptomatic of the illness. Ed does not like being challenged
or being told it is no longer needed or welcome. Ed will do
anything to hang on as long as possible. Losing your temper or
your patience will reinforce what Ed is already yelling inside the
sufferer's head: 'You are not worth their time and effort – they
don't understand and don't really care.'

> 'It's really important to visualize that your child is separate
> from the illness. Your child is still in there, but the illness
> has a louder voice than you inside their mind at the
> moment and it is making them afraid to eat. You must
> insist on talking only to your child, encourage them, and
> do not engage with their illness. Ignore it.'
>
> *– Father*

## Just get better!

 **@friend** You can't keep doing this – we can't
keep rushing you off to hospital when you say
you are in danger and need urgent medical
help, only to have you refuse treatment and
abuse us when we get you there!

**@Ed** *You know there's nothing wrong with you – stop being an attention seeker!*

**@adultsufferer** *I'm scared. Am I the only one who feels this way? I don't know if I have a diagnosable illness or if I am just plain weak. I know I need help to beat this thing that has taken over my mind – but I fear the doctors will put me into a mental institution. I don't want to be talked about and treated like a crazy person. Inside I'm still me, the 'A' student and mother of two beautiful little children.*

---

**@friend** I've had enough of your stupid moods. You only do this to get attention. You never accept the treatment you are offered and you throw our support back in our faces. Until you get your act together we are through.

**@Ed** *Your friends are sick of you. Who can blame them, you are a total screw up.*

**@adultsufferer** *I knew my friends would abandon me eventually. I knew I didn't really matter to them. Fact is, I don't deserve them.*

**@survivor** It got to where I could no longer talk to my family – they didn't want to know about this 'illness' any more. But my friends stood by me. They helped carry me through.

---

**@sufferer** *I get so stressed when we go out, I am literally sick before I get through the front door. Mum has to get me a change of clothes. I just hate going out – I wish she wouldn't make me go. I yell and complain to try to get her to give up – but all she does is get cranky herself. But it's funny, when we get to where we are going, like to my grandparents, it's never as bad as I fear. I'm glad, then, that she has made me go. I have fun.*

**@mum** She can be such a pain. She whines and complains and yells until she is sick on her best clothes. It's always the same routine. But when we finally get there, it's like a switch has flicked and she's fine. Like it's OK for her just to forget all the crap she's just put me through. She ruins the outing for me every time – I'm all flustered and uptight, and people notice this, while little Miss gets to act like nothing happened!

---

**@mum** We had time to spare, so went window shopping before our therapy appointment – and the little rotter was as happy as happy. She has control over this so-called illness, you know. Either that, or we are the problem. She acts fine when she is out but plays up something terrible at home.

**@therapist** I know it looks that way, but she doesn't have control over this, and you are not the problem. The window shopping was a lovely distraction, that's all. It gave her a moment to be her true self: a small respite from the torment of the Ed voice.

---

**@mum** You've been lying to me and exercising in your room when the doctor has told you not to. Why can't you just behave yourself?

**@Ed** *She's spying on you – she's out to ruin everything you've worked for. You have to be more careful to hide from her.*

**@sufferer** *I want to please Mum and the doctor and not let them down, but I must do my exercises.*

---

**@friend** Well, if you already know you are too thin, why do you keep starving yourself and running for hours on end? Your behaviour does not make sense.

**@adultsufferer** *She thinks that weight loss is my aim, but it's only a side-effect of being good at all my rituals. And I need these rituals to keep everything under control. Otherwise I can't get through the day. It's how I cope with life.*

## Patience is a virtue

**@sufferer** Why don't you just stuff me in a mental institution then if I'm so awful?

 **@mum** No – we are going to stand by you no matter what. We want to look after you at home where you have our love 24/7. Better than being an inpatient in the hospital where the staff may not understand that behind all those eating disorder behaviours is a lovely girl.

**@Ed** *Quick! Push her away. She's trying to trick you. She only wants to make you eat. And then you will fail at all your hard work!*

**@sufferer** Yeah, well I wish you were all dead. And I don't care that you spent three hours preparing that meal. I won't eat it. I can't.

**@mum** We know that you are still in there, suppressed by your illness, and we are not giving up until we have you back and your eating disorder is gone – for good. You will eat this meal.

**@sufferer** *I'm not worth their effort – I'm a horrible person – why do they still love me? I want to please them, but I can't. I'm too afraid to eat.*

**@sufferer** When they made me go to hospital I hated it – I was so scared. I tried to get at my parents by saying things like 'If you love me you will take me home' and worse – I threatened a number of times to kill myself. Then I ripped all my clothes up. I was so angry, I lost control.

**@mum** All we could do was to let her say all her terrible stuff to us and reassure her that we knew it was the illness striking out because it wasn't happy she was being helped. We went out and bought her some new clothes and a quilt for her hospital bed to make it more home-like. At the end of her stay she was able to take this quilt home and it gave her comfort to keep it with her.

---

**@sufferer** I was terrified. Every week they would weigh me. And every week my weight would either stay the same or go down (which I loved). But that would mean they would add more food into my meal plan. I couldn't deal with this. So I came up with the idea of hiding weights in my clothes. I thought it would help – but Dad guessed and told the therapist and I know they were all disappointed in me.

**@dad** She became so devious! She hid weights from the hems of curtains in her bra and socks. But I'm an anaesthetist, used to judging body weight. I could tell she had not gained weight. She tried to trick us when all we were trying to do was help her – but we understood that it was Ed, not her. We keep those weights as a reminder of how manipulative Ed can be! Thank goodness today we can all laugh.

---

**@sufferer** I want to do recovery properly this time, and I think part of that means getting to the BMI [body mass index] recommended by my doctor rather than staying at the lowest medically acceptable weight. I have to give it a try.

**@nurse** That BMI is far too ambitious for you: you've been ill for a long time and will probably never fully recover.

**@Ed** *You are a lost cause. You will never recover. No one believes in you.*

**@sufferer** *She's saying that there is little hope for me and I am wasting my time. Thank goodness I have recovered sufficiently to know that I won't listen to her!*

---

**@sufferer** I am wondering if I will see any of the therapists during this hospital admission?

**@nurse** No, you had therapy last time you were a patient here and you relapsed, so we will just monitor your weight this time.

**@Ed** *The therapist doesn't want to see you. You're just a waste of his time.*

**@sufferer** *I'm not worth the therapist's time and effort because I didn't recover as a patient a year ago – nobody cares about the fact that the previous time I hadn't wanted to get better, and this time I do!*

## A new me?

Weight restoration is one of several stages of recovery of anorexia. The terrifying moments are not over yet. Besides weight restoration, recovery requires sufferers to let go of ED behaviours and thoughts. It is not an easy process.

 **@dad** Honey, why do you always wear those old baggy clothes? Surely you will feel better if you put on that pretty dress. Take a little pride in your appearance. You'll feel happier.

**@Ed** *Why? Because you're a hopeless fat pig – that's why.*

**@sufferer** *I don't deserve anything nicer than these baggy clothes that I've been wearing for 12 months. I am so worthless. I will wear only these clothes until I lose more weight.*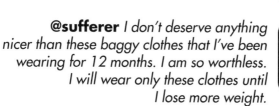

**@mum** I know it was our idea to allow the doctors to insert the nasogastric tube and you said you hated both it and us – but now you seem almost proud of it. You would not go to the shopping mall before, but now you have the tube, you are happy to wander about in public, and you seem almost happy that people are looking at you.

**@teensufferer** *The only way I can let people see me is with the tube in – I want them all to know that being this fat is NOT MY FAULT! It is being forced on me. I'm not lazy and weak.*

**@sufferer** *My therapist says: no exercising. I can't even run for five minutes without the Ed thoughts ramping up, compelling me to do more – the triggers go off and I have to do a five-hour slog. It's hard because I hate sitting still, but I do want to be free of this horrid illness. I will do some needlepoint as a distraction.*

**@Ed** *It's not healthy to be this sedentary. Everyone is supposed to exercise – it's normal behaviour. What's not normal is this lazy sitting on the couch thing you've got going. It's pathetic. You are making excuses for being a slob. You will get fat – and you will regret it – because you will have to start your weight loss all over again.*

 **@survivor** Creating new interests like a hobby is an excellent step towards regaining you.

**@sufferer** Everyone is being amazing –
even my personal trainer wants to know
how best she can support my recovery and
has been in touch with my Ed therapist.

**@Ed** *Honestly, you are a grown woman –
why do you need everyone babysitting you
like this – you should be able to fix this
yourself. You get more pathetic every day.*

 **@survivor** Think of recovery like a child
learning to ride a bike with trainer wheels –
likewise we need to maintain a network of
support in Ed recovery until we are sure we
can carry on without falling over and, even
after letting go, remain vigilant.

# 9

—

# Food

—

*No one ever climbed a mountain by standing at the bottom
and deciding to jump to the top. Every mountain climb is
made up of thousands of steps and each step is necessary.*

People with anorexia may suffer from anosognosia, a condition in
which they seem unaware that they have an illness or disability.
They may be starving but unable to acknowledge this. Even when
they have the ability to recognize they have an eating disorder,
and want to recover, the effects of the illness do not automatically
go away.

Sometimes the insight that their behaviour, thoughts and diet
are not normal can make the sufferer feel worse about themselves
as they do not have sufficient self-awareness or skills to address the
thoughts or behaviour. Anxiety and fear around food are among
the most challenging of eating disorder symptoms to overcome.

## Obsession

Fear of food is exacerbated in treatment when the main focus of
everything the sufferer does now revolves around three meals and
three snacks a day. Being inundated with nutritional information
and instructions can feel like a loss of independence. The sense
of comfort and control that restriction, purging, exercise or
bingeing provided in an otherwise out-of-control life is often
now potentially replaced in other areas of life.

**@mum** Her obsession with food extended far beyond the dinner table. Every time someone went to the pantry or the fridge, she wanted to know what food we were taking out. I would stand at the pantry door, checking to see what I needed to buy at the supermarket to restock, and would sense that my daughter had snuck up quietly, and was watching me from behind. It was creepy.

**@sufferer** My only thoughts were about food. The more I couldn't eat it, the more I needed to be around it. I needed to read about food, to see food, to shop for food and help prepare food. I had to know exactly how much food there was in the house, how many calories were in it, and who was eating what. I don't know why. I just needed to know.

---

 **@dietician** You are not eating enough for the amount of activity you do – I want you to follow an easy food plan. You will need scales and a measuring jug to ensure you have the right amounts.

**@sufferer** *Ooh, I never thought of measuring my food! Now I can really keep track of how much I eat – and I'm sure to feel better if I measure just a \*little\* bit less each day!*

 **@survivor** Someone actively trying to recover may find the act of measuring reassuring, but be cautious: it is tempting to use it as a means to eat less. Never eat less: a good dietician will start you off with what they believe is a sensible but manageable amount or, in other words, the minimum.

---

 **@mum** Why is your schoolwork suddenly such a big deal? It won't matter if you don't do exactly three hours' homework tonight. You are exhausted! Please stop studying and go to bed.

*@teensufferer I have to feel like I'm doing something right. I can't do any less than three hours because that's what I've put on my must-do schedule. I'll fail if I fall behind and then what will be the point of trying to recover?*

 **@experiencedcarer** Many people with eating disorders find they need to make rules and stick to them for fear of 'failing' or being 'bad'. When deprived of the ability to control food intake and exercise, the rule-making tendency may pop up in other aspects of life. For instance, the drive to get good marks, while admirable, may become another eating disorder trait. When in doubt, talk with your therapist.

## Avoidance

Endless meal times are one of Ed's powerful weapons: the illness seems to count on carers giving up, becoming distracted, getting angry and storming out. To win, all you need to do is wait a little longer than Ed. Aim to out-sit Ed every time – because this is what it takes. And although you are human and tempers will fray, voices will be raised and at some point crockery may fly, every time you out-sit Ed you weaken its voice and the habit of eating grows stronger.

*Telephone conversation:*

**@mum** It's 2pm and we are still waiting for our daughter to eat two spoonfuls of her breakfast cereal. How long did you say we have to sit and wait with her for each meal?

**@therapist** You have to sit by your child at the table a little longer than the eating disorder. If she misses classes and her afternoon job at the pharmacy, so be it. Don't give in to the illness.

---

**@mum** Food in this house is not negotiable – you need to eat your dinner.

**@teensufferer** *I have worked hard to get slim and my parents want to take it all away from me. Being slim is the most important thing in the world to me. I want to lose more weight and, instead, they are stuffing me. I hate them. It's so unfair!*

**@experiencedcarer** People with anorexia are often incapable of understanding that their illness is dominating and manipulating their thoughts. Carers can help during the initial and difficult refeeding phase by learning skills to challenge and defuse the illness on the sick person's behalf.

---

**@teensufferer** Oh, I can see you are pleased that I'm getting fat. Why don't you all pat yourselves on the back and do a high five? Yay for you and your stupid FBT. Yep, you all win and I lose. Whoopee. I hate you.

 **@mum** Ever since we started Maudsley FBT our daughter has found it helpful to blame us for making her eat. We don't care. As long as she eats we don't care how she justifies it.

 **@survivor** Blaming my parents seemed the easiest way to get the food in my mouth. It was their fault – they were making me eat. Having them sit beside me at the table kept my Ed voice from tormenting me too much – I just kept promising myself that I would lose the weight again later.

**@teensufferer** DON'T WATCH ME! It's so unfair…*tears* *sobbing* I can't eat this while you sit and look at me – please, please leave me alone.

 **@mum** When we started to sit with our daughter during meals her illness became trapped; it might have been outwitting our daughter, but not us. We were taking it on. There was no chance to not eat, and no chance to purge after meals. At first our daughter was very angry but gradually she stopped fighting us and began to relax and eat more easily at meal times. Diversion helped, like reading out loud the favourite childhood classics and doing word puzzles.

**@survivor** When Mum and Dad first started sitting with me at the dinner table I was terrified. I could no longer hide my food, or purge the meals afterwards, with them watching me 24/7. They were relentless in their vigilance. But soon I realized that, although I was gaining weight, it wasn't like 20 kilograms a day, and I started to think I didn't want to go back to that dark place where I had been; I was starting to re-engage in life and was thinking I could beat this thing.

---

 **@dad** Just eat the food! You know we are going to sit here until you eat all the food on your plate. Stop trying to scoot it on to the floor and stop trying to hide it. We know the tricks that your illness gets up to.

**@teensufferer** It's not fair. The therapist says I am not allowed to play sport and therefore I will not eat this food.

*Only fat people don't play sport. I don't play sport now – so I am fat. Everyone must be able to see that. I will not eat the food.*

 **@dad** As soon as you return to a healthy weight you can play sport again. You will risk long-term damage to your body if you exercise right now. First and foremost, your body needs refeeding. The sooner you eat, the sooner you can resume sport.

---

**@teensufferer** I hate you. You can't make me eat this crap. I know you've loaded it with extra fat because you want me to be fat so you can win. I'll never let you win.

**@experiencedcarer** The idea that the illness and my son are separate entities and that no one is to blame for the illness helps me enormously. I am not to blame, and my son is not to blame. Also I know that it is not my son who is acting out so aggressively. It is the illness. I can accept and put up with the abuse now I know it is not him speaking.

---

**@clinician** Your daughter needs your help to reach the stage where she wants to recover and is capable of resuming responsibility for eating. Until this time, you need to supervise the eating of every meal and snack.

**@mum** I don't want to force her to do something she isn't ready to do. I don't want her to hate me.

**@survivor** I just couldn't choose recovery. I couldn't do it on my own. I couldn't see there was anything wrong. I needed my parents to do it for me. Yes, I hated them at the time, but now I realize they were my greatest resource. My parents stood up to Ed on my behalf until I recovered sufficiently to take over the responsibility of feeding myself.

---

**@nana** You will eat this sandwich for me, won't you, sweetheart?

**@teensufferer** No, grandmother, not you, too! Why is everyone against me? Mum told you to say that – she told you to trick me into eating that sandwich, didn't she?

 **@experiencedcarer** She was such a sweet child, always eager to please, before this illness developed. I had to understand that the anorexia made my granddaughter behave very differently, not to take her outbursts personally and not to give up trying to get past the illness and through to her.

---

 **@mum** Our daughter trusts no one and doesn't feel safe from Ed's voice anywhere… she pleads with us to leave her alone, so her life can end and she can be at peace.

 **@experiencedcarer** Although this sounds awful, chances are your daughter is giving you your script, for what she most needs to hear from you when she's suffering is: 'Trust us,' 'You are safe with us,' 'This is safe,' and 'This food is what you need to eat to find peace.'

---

 **@dad** How dare you speak to your mother like that? Stop being rude and eat your food – now!

**@sufferer** This casserole has fat globules floating everywhere – it tastes like slop and I won't eat it!

*I can't eat this food – I feel sick and disgusting for even looking it. Dad doesn't understand. If I eat I'll get fat. I don't deserve to eat ever again. I am ruining everything.*

 **@experiencedcarer** The FBT therapist explained that the abuse pouring from my daughter's mouth was driven by her illness and not by her. I learned to ignore the expletives and say, 'Put the potato on your fork, put it in your mouth,' over and over, quietly, for hours on end, if necessary.

---

 **@teacher** Now your mum and I have agreed that I will sit with you at morning tea to support you and make sure you eat the food she has packed for you.

**@tweensufferer** Yes, I know, Mum told me.

 **@teacher** OK, so let's see what Mum has packed.

**@tweensufferer** Urgh, orange cake. She knows I hate orange cake.

**@teacher** And wow! That is one seriously big piece of cake. It looks delicious, though.

**@experiencedcarer** Ed will misinterpret any comment about food as a criticism or a reason not to eat it. The student was already trying to avoid eating the cake by talking about not liking it – but the teacher's comment on the size of the piece spoke so directly to Ed this meal was over before it started. The student heard: 'If you eat that enormous cake you are a pig.' Avoid being drawn into conversation about the food, especially when you are not the primary caregiver.

---

**@mum** The most distressing thing is to hear words from my dear daughter that make no sense. They aren't random – they have a pattern – but they don't seem to be in the same reality as we are living.

**@experiencedcarer** You can learn to translate:

'I hate this food' can mean:
'I'm afraid of this food.'

'I hate you' can mean: 'I'm frightened and you are the only one I trust enough to flail at, because you won't leave me.'

'I don't like potatoes any more' can be interpreted as: 'I need you to challenge me by serving me potatoes – not today, but soon.'

## Trust

The desire to load your child up with calories at every available opportunity is overwhelming – this is understandable. When looking at your child disappearing before your eyes you will do whatever it takes to hang on to them. For some children this will work – but most are watching your every move. Very little in the way of extra calories can be 'snuck' into their food without them knowing. If your child is the sort to notice every little thing then you have an extra fine line to walk. Holding on to their trust, so that they really believe (even if they will never admit it) that you are helping them, is vital. Often a third person such as a dietician or therapist can suggest strategies for building this trust and helping your child put any perceived breaches of trust into perspective.

**@sufferer** I can't eat anything my mum makes for me. She keeps lying to me about what's in my food. I mean, I saw her plop a huge dollop of cream in the mashed potato. We always use milk. I can't trust her.

 **@dietician** You must stop trying to trick your son. You need to be open about everything you do.

 **@mum** But I want to get as many calories into him as possible. The more calories the better, surely.

 **@dietician** Yes, but now he knows you are trying to add extra ingredients in a sneaky way. Your child has to know he can trust you if he is going to eat the meals you prepare. Trust is vital in taking a stand against the eating disorder. Otherwise the sly Ed picks up on it, creates confusion and inhibits recovery.

**@mum** I tell you what, if you eat an ice cream while we are out shopping, you won't have to drink the regular milkshake when we get home.

**@teensufferer** *shoulder shrug* OK.

*Fine, to make her happy I will eat the ice cream; best to get it over and done with.*

*Back home...*

 **@mum** I know what I said when shopping, but I have decided you still have to drink the milkshake.

**@teensufferer** *She lied! *sobs* I can't believe she tricked me like that. I'm all alone in this. I can never trust her again* ☹

 **@experiencedcarer** Understandably the mother is seizing every opportunity to help her daughter gain weight. However, cajoling with false promises backfires. Consistency is crucial in beating the anorexia. Weeks of recovery work can be lost when you break your word as Ed grabs it and says: 'See, you can't trust her, you are safer with me.'

---

 **@mum** I know the nasogastric tube is challenging for you, but the doctor has only increased your energy intake today by a tiny, tiny amount. You won't even notice it.

**@teensufferer** *It's not a matter of how tiny the amount is! It's more. That's all that counts. It's more. It's being forced into me and will make me heavier. That's all there is to this conversation.*

**@experiencedcarer** Even a gram or two can seem humongous and spark fear in a person with anorexia. Any increase in energy intake or change to routine is frightening. Be patient and provide reassurance.

## Nothing to see here, move along

Carers, families and friends must encourage and remind their loved one they have done nothing wrong by having an eating disorder and there is no cause for shame. However, in some situations, covering it up or acting as though there is nothing wrong can be the right strategy in challenging the symptoms.

**@husband** Oh c'mon honey, the waitress can't stand at our table all night waiting for you to order – hurry up and choose your meal. Everyone else has done so, already.

**@sufferer** *I can't even look at the menu. There's nothing listed that I can eat. There are too many choices. I don't want to be here and now everyone's looking at me. I want to go home!*

**@experiencedcarer** My wife and I have a code word so that she can let me know if she starts to feel anxious while looking at the menu. I then choose a meal for her without drawing attention to her. This way her illness can't blame her for the menu choice; I take the pressure off.

**@mum** Oh good girl, you're eating your dinner before I needed to remind you it's meal time. You are making such good progress.

**@Ed** *Are you sure you can't shovel that food in any faster?*

**@sufferer** *Oh no! What have I done? I was hungry when I got home from school and started to eat before I realized what I was doing. I'm so weak and pathetic! Stop eating RIGHT NOW!*

 **@experiencedcarer** Don't draw attention to your daughter eating. She is most likely feeling self-conscious about it and struggling with guilt. Rather than comment on her eating, follow up the meal with a pleasant distracting activity (such as a card game or discussing a TV show while doing the dishes) to help dispel the torment she feels after the meal.

# 10

## Relationships

*Sometimes you don't need someone to fix the problem;
you need someone to hold you while you cry.*

Relationships can take a battering when an eating disorder develops. Everyone in the family is affected. Extended family relationships also are tested because people who don't live with the illness 24/7 have difficulty understanding its severity.

> 'Concern and compassion flowed into our home when I was diagnosed with breast cancer. After all, I hadn't chosen to have this potentially deadly illness. I received flowers, phone calls and get well cards, and casseroles landed on my front doorstep. But as for my daughter, who had anorexia, we might as well have said we were washing our dog. People believed she chose to have her illness. But she did not choose anorexia, any more than I chose breast cancer.'
>
> *– Mother*

Eating disorders seem to thrive on isolating the person with the illness from the people they love and driving a wedge between people who hitherto have cared deeply for each other.

Couples are tested, too. While two is company, Ed makes three and crowds the relationship. The partner without the ED often takes on the role of carer. Their own needs may go unmet and their efforts may not be appreciated. The person with the illness is resentful at being told to 'eat what's on your plate' as if they are a child; no wonder then, that romantic feelings wilt.

Relationships with friends can wane as excuse after excuse is given to avoid social gatherings, especially where food is served. Relationships in the workplace can also feel the strain. Mood swings – depending on how much Ed is ranting and raving within – add to the mix.

## Parent–child relationships

**@teensufferer** If Dad cared about me he wouldn't be so busy at work all the time. I know he's avoiding me. I don't want us to live with him any more. I want you and me to live alone.

**@mum** The eating disorder is not your dad's fault at all – and you saying things like that hurt him deeply. He has to work extra hours to pay the medical bills. And no, I'm not going to leave Dad – he's part of our family and we love him.

**@teensufferer** *So that's why he detests me – he resents me for causing him to work longer hours – and you love him more than me! I don't want to be with ANY of you! You ALL hate me! This is so unfair!*

**@experiencedcarer** Sometimes everything you say seems to add fuel to Ed's fire. At such times, if diversion to another topic does not work, time out can be a wise option. Above all, avoiding responding to the eating disorder talk.

**@mum** We're taking you home from college so that we can take on the responsibility of feeding you. You clearly need help and can't do it yourself.

*@Ed Oh no! Panic stations! You'll never be able to keep going if they are watching you. You have to listen to me! Yell at them and refuse them. Quickly!*

**@unistudentsufferer** Do you seriously think I'm an infant? I do not need to be babied – and I certainly don't need to be fed. I will not let you.

*Why do I say things like that when for such a long time this is what I have wanted? I know I can't do this alone – I need someone to insist that I eat; to stand up to these powerful thoughts that torment me – but somehow I just can't give in and let them.*

 **@experiencedcarer** Relief can be almost audible when parents negotiate with their child to take control. Importantly, the parents need to be stronger than Ed.

---

 **@dad** She was literally rolling around in the mud outside screaming at the top of her lungs – I mean, who does that? That was not my daughter.

**@sufferer** I was so revolting. I had been forced to eat for weeks on end. I could feel all the fat clinging to my body. The food stuck to my mouth and the inside of my throat.

Nothing could make it go away, and my parents persisted in making me eat – I felt an urge to be as disgusting as I felt.

---

**@teensufferer** Don't you see how bad you make me feel when you yell back at me, and the worst is when you cry! Why can't you just be patient with me the way the therapist said you should be?

 **@mum** I'm sorry that I lost the plot and shouted. I cried because I am tired. I love you but I hate your illness. I am only human. I have been sitting here for four hours, waiting for you to eat your meal.

---

 **@mum** Your cousin, who you loved to play with as a child, has died and yet you haven't dropped a tear.

**@sufferer** *I honestly feel no emotion whatsoever. My emotions are numbed. All I care about is my total number of calories for the day. This is the only way I can get through the day and the intensity consumes me.*

---

 **@mum** No, honey, I can't give you money to go buy another new cell phone cover.

**@sufferer** You hate me. This isn't fair!

 **@mum** No, I don't hate you. I explained that if you kept all of your therapy appointments this past week that I'd buy the new cover for you. Unfortunately you skipped your dietician appointment.

**@sufferer** It's obvious: you hate me and don't want me to get well.

 **@experiencedcarer** There is no winning this – Ed is determined that I hate my daughter and while she is undernourished there is no way to convince her differently. She is unable to differentiate between me setting boundaries as a mother and Ed's banter that she is unworthy. For trust to develop I must keep my word and be consistent.

---

 **@mum** My daughter says her Ed voice is loudest at night and makes her get out of bed and exercise while we are asleep. I'm wondering if I should sleep in her room to keep a vigil.

 **@experiencedcarer** I slept with my tall daughter in a double bed for five months! And I am not small so it was all a bit cosy. She complained but in her sleep would grab my hand and put it round her waist. Rarely now she will suddenly say on a bad day: 'Mum, you're not thinking of sleeping in my bed are you?' This is the code for: 'I need you to sleep with me tonight and protect me from thoughts of exercise.'

## Perspectives

**@sufferer** My mother is too overprotective. She likes to keep me under her control. If I say I've already eaten, and don't want dinner tonight, she pushes until I get upset and angry. She loves this because then she can throw it back in my face with 'See, that is your eating disorder talking.' She's the one doing it on purpose.

 **@mum** If I push her too much, if I challenge her fears, I see her demeanour change and I know that it is no longer her talking to me – but her eating disorder. I point this out and her eating disorder hates being exposed.

**@survivor** At the end of the day, the person and the eating disorder are one and the same. As recovery proceeds and life engagement increases, the remnants of Ed may reappear from time to time, especially at times of stress. Constant vigilance by both sufferer and carer will help minimize risk of relapse.

---

 **@mum** The four-hour car ride home from therapy is usually the worst, because our daughter is upset at her weight gain and issues brought up in therapy. Her illness fights against this confrontation and there is no escaping it in the car. At home I can go into another room and try to emotionally detach myself but in the car I'm stuck.

**@teensufferer** *I hate the car ride home. My heart is pounding; adrenalin is still rushing through my body, I feel physically sick and exhausted. I need to be left alone after a session; instead, I'm stuck in the car for four hours with everyone looking at me and thinking I'm such a bitch for refusing to say a word at therapy. I know they blame me for making them drive there and back. They think I'm not trying, but I am. So I yell at them. I've got so much stuff going on in my head.*

**@experiencedcarer** There is no doubt about it – tackling Ed is exhausting work. Both carers and sufferers can need time out.

---

**@mum** My son hates it when I talk about his illness to my friends. I try to explain that I am not talking about him – I am talking about his anorexia and he is not his anorexia. I know that exposure makes his Ed voice very uncomfortable. But I will not hide it. I will not be ashamed that my son has an illness that is not his fault. And I will not stop having conversations that I find helpful – because I need support too. It's amazing – when I open up and share, many people start to share their experiences too.

**@sufferer** She gossips and bitches about me to her friends and I hate it. I'm not here for their entertainment. She has no right to discuss me like I am some sort of freak show. She is not allowed to talk about me and that's final.

**@experiencedcarer** ED can be very isolating and carers can feel better sharing their load with others. However, it is wise to choose a safe, respectful and supportive environment; one that won't offend the sufferer. A litmus test is to ask yourself, would you like to be talked about in this way?

---

**@teensufferer** *My family is worried about me, and I can see they are putting their lives on hold to help me get better. I can eat this doughnut for them. I can do this because my parents are right by my side and this helps me feel safe. I am so glad they have not given up on me.*

**@Ed** *Your family is so controlling. They love this hovering and watching game – it makes them feel important. They hate that you have opinions about your life and the way you want to live. Show them how strong you are – don't eat this!*

**@survivor** Ed thrives on casting doubt and the support of family and friends is vital in ongoing recovery. Each time Ed is ignored, the true self has opportunity to strengthen.

---

**@tweensufferer** I can't eat at school – it's so humiliating. I feel everyone is looking at me, and thinking what a slob I am.

**@mum** I try to appeal to her rational side – to focus on things that I see are important, like health and safety and getting stronger. She throws it back in my face with comments like 'Who cares, no one will like me if I'm fat.'

**@therapist** Another way is to appeal to what will motivate your daughter – like improving her relationships with her friends. Point out how her eating disorder is getting in the way of her enjoyment of these social interactions. Describe what life can be like beyond Ed and encourage her friends to share their everyday happenings so that she feels included and accepted.

---

*In therapy session:*

**@mum** Dad and I are proud of how well you have done in school despite missing many classes for your therapy appointments. We know the grades aren't what you want, but we think that you are doing great!

**@teensufferer** *wails* See, she thinks my grades are hopeless too! Anything less than the top of the class is a failure.

**@therapist** Well, that's not what I heard your mum say. Let's talk about what you heard.

**@experiencedcarer** This breakthrough conversation was a relief, as it highlighted clearly to our daughter and us that her ED was distorting everything we said. It was like Ed had finally made a mistake and revealed itself in public.

## Sibling relationships

 **@olderbrother** I wrote you a poem.

**@tweensufferer** It's beautiful. It really is. I love it so much.

 **@olderbrother** Thanks – I mean what I wrote.

**@tweensufferer** I could never write anything this good. You are so much better at everything than me.

 **@olderbrother** Oh man. You know, you're a fun kid, but seriously your illness is really boring. You bring it into everything.

**@oldersister** I hate that yelling and screaming is now commonplace in our house. Can't we just go back to the way we were before? Before all this worry about food and weight. I'm trying to study for my final exams and my sister gets all the attention. It's hard to find a quiet spot in the house.

**@teensufferer** *Ha! I would love to be back at school like my sister but I'm scared to go out of the house. I don't want to be like this. I am terrified of eating anything but the same food, in the same way, every day – that's why I yell when my parents put more food on my plate. It's not because I want to make a scene or a fuss – I'm just so scared of any change, any change at all.*

## Perspectives

Ed will use anything it can to isolate the sufferer – and driving a wedge of resentment between siblings is a common tactic. Maintaining a strong bond between siblings is important, but often the healthy siblings feel forgotten when another child in the family is walking a line between life and death:

'I often felt overlooked and excluded. People basically assumed that I did not play a role in my family's struggles, as if I did not also have to deal with them.'

'Friends of my parents would always say, "Look after your mother and father, and sister for us," but none ever asked them to look after me.'

'I felt frustrated, when my sister would be asked eight times to sit down to dinner. I just wanted her to be normal and sit down like the rest of us.'

'I felt a bit angry with her, for always taking up our mother's time, and felt scared, as I knew little about her illness.'

'I try and ignore my sister's bulimia – it's easier for me this way as she is not ready to confront it.'

'I didn't like to put my problems on our parents – they had enough to do helping my sister. Sometimes I cried myself to sleep, worrying that "the worst" would happen.'

'The biggest scare was when my sister asked us to let her die and I found her in her bedroom at home with a dressing gown cord around her neck.'

'I often feel isolated and excluded.'

'The worst part is the yelling and fighting at meal times, with my parents trying to persuade my sister to eat.'

'I feel forgotten at home and increasingly isolated at school.'

'As a result of my sister having anorexia, I have matured faster than many of my friends and therefore have lost a lot of common ground with them. All they want to talk about is the "weekend", either the one just past or the one coming up. They have such carefree lives. Dad has rigged up a punching bag at home so I can get rid of my frustration.'

'I am devoted to the role of being my sister's friend during treatment but sometimes feel I am betraying our parents, as they do not know a lot of my sister's secrets.'

'The time away from school for family-based treatment plus the effort of completing homework, amid the yelling and shouting during the extended meal times, means I often do not pass work in on time. I am usually a week or two late, and some of the teachers are not understanding.'

'I have started noticing disordered eating habits among friends, but at the same time I want to block it out. I have had enough of it at home.'

'I feel annoyed watching her eat chocolate bars and knowing what she will do next because I know what her bulimia makes her do. This makes it difficult to be around her for long.'

'I had no idea she was so sick until we began family-based treatment and then I freaked out. I feared she might die.'

'Whenever I answer the family telephone, everyone asks "How is your sister?" because she has the eating disorder, but they never ask after me.'

## Partner relationships

**@husband** Why do you shut me out? We both know you have an eating disorder, so why can't you accept the help and support I am offering you?

**@sufferer** You think you know everything, going to those stupid carer support classes and talking to others about me. But you don't know anything. There's nothing wrong with me – I just need to be stronger and stop letting myself down. I know what I am doing – and you need to stop standing in my way.

**@Ed** *He's so embarrassed by you – it isn't like he doesn't have enough on his plate already, now he has to look after you like an infant. He's going to leave you. You are not the strong amazing person he thought he was marrying. You are a fake.*

**@husband** Sometimes I feel like you're not even in the room with me. It's like your body is here, but your mind is somewhere else. I can be talking to you for five minutes and you don't even hear me!

**@sufferer** *How do I tell him that I have something like 47 arguments going on in my head at the same time – I just can't hear him over all the noise. It's exhausting.*

---

 **@boyfriend** The doctor says you must eat three meals and three snacks a day and remember that he suggested I sit beside you while you eat to keep you company.

**@Ed** *He's trying to control you. He's trying to watch your every move so he can take all this hard work away from you.*

**@sufferer** You are not my father, you are my boyfriend, so support and love me, but don't tell me what to do.

 **@boyfriend** You are special to me so I'll sit with you. I know you would do the same for me.

---

 **@husband** Why can't you eat the same nutritious meals that you serve up for the children and me? You would feel much better if you did and so would I.

**@Ed** *Why can't you just be a sensible grown-up for once? Well, because you have no self-control that's why!*

**@sufferer** I really like a plate of vegetables. It's all I need to feel good, really.

*I wish I could eat a nice roast dinner with my family but I'm terrified that if I eat an ordinary meal of meat, vegetables and gravy, I will binge myself stupid for the rest of the day. I mean, I would not know the exact number of calories in the gravy. So my plan for the entire day would be thrown out of whack.*

---

**@middleagedsufferer** The man in my life is loyal and trustworthy and loves me dearly. He wants to marry me. My quandary is he doesn't excite me. I don't feel any passion. I don't know if this is because he doesn't appeal to my Ed, or doesn't appeal to ME. This could be my chance to be in a safe and secure relationship and I'm about to blow it.

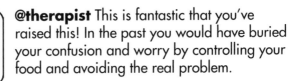

**@therapist** This is fantastic that you've raised this! In the past you would have buried your confusion and worry by controlling your food and avoiding the real problem.

**@survivor** After focusing on food for decades, attempting to face relationship issues as they come up instead of counting calories is initially a huge challenge. Learning to face these issues and getting in touch with feelings is an important step towards recovery and rebuilding a social life.

# Relationships that Ed likes

Sadly not all partners are supportive and caring. This is largely because Ed thrives on manipulating relationships. Often people with eating disorders find themselves attracted to people who treat them in the same controlling way that Ed does. Initially partners may seem charismatic and exciting, but turn out to be abusive and neglectful. Persisting through therapy to find and believe in your true self can lead to the realization and acceptance that you really do deserve better.

 **@boyfriend** You are a weirdo and schizo. Do you know what it's like for me having to live with a woman like you? All my friends tell me you're nuts and I should just walk out. You have five minds in one and are the most negative woman I have ever met.

*@sufferer He's right. I've been battling my eating disorder for so long I have no idea who I am. I know I have mood swings. I deserve all that he says.*

 **@survivor** Ed can form powerful attachments to charismatic but controlling men, making you impervious to the advice of friends, family and health carers that they are an entirely unsuitable match. Living on the edge of life with excitement that is potentially dangerous and continually chaotic can seem preferable to facing the pain of alienation due to the eating disorder. The challenge is to have the courage to be true to you, instead of Ed. The support of therapist and friends can help achieve this ideal, and open the door to a relationship and a life that is safe, secure, stable AND exciting.

---

 **@husband** I don't know who you are any more. You're mouthy and rude and quite frankly I don't like it.

**@sufferer** I'm not being rude – I just don't happen to agree with you and I think it's only fair I say so.

 **@husband** It's that stupid therapist isn't it – she's put you up to all this crap. Seriously, woman, if you don't knock it off I'm out of here.

 **@survivor** It had never occurred to me before that he wouldn't like the 'new improved' me. But he didn't. And I had to make the difficult realization that I did like the new me, and had outgrown my relationship with him.

---

 **@partner** You're never home. Dinner is never ready and my clothes are never washed.

**@sufferer** Therapy is taking up a lot of my time, plus we agreed that having a part-time job would be good for me. And it is – I'm happy. I'm starting to live again.

**@partner** Yeah, but I didn't know it was going to ruin my life.

**@survivor** Significant others are affected by the eating disorder, too, and adjustments become necessary as recovery proceeds. Recovery creates an opportunity for self-growth in everyone involved.

## Carer relationships

**@mum** So you 'get' that I have breast cancer and that it is not my fault, but you can't grasp that my daughter's anorexia is not her fault?

**@adultfriend** Be fair, cancer is a real illness, a very serious one. Honestly, your daughter needs to stop being selfish and take better care of you. You are the one who is sick. She's just looking for attention.

**@experiencedcarer** I had to learn that some people are incapable or persistently unwilling to accept that eating disorders are not a choice. Right then, I did need support and had no energy for anyone who could not provide that. So that friend went by the wayside.

---

**@mum** She has got you twisted around her little finger. You think just because you see her eating meals at your house that she's fine. You don't see the whole story. I have to make her sit at the table. I have to make sure she eats her meals and snacks every day and put up with her tantrums.

 **@grandma** No dear, you're too hard on her. Remember, she's just a little girl. She needs your love and compassion, not your 'tough love'. She doesn't eat because you push her too hard – she always eats for me.

*@**sufferer** I save calories by eating less at home so that I can eat a meal at Grandma's house. When we get home, I go for a run and work it off. I don't like others knowing about my illness.*

# 11

## Sense of Self

*It would be nice for once to look in the mirror
and see my personality instead of my skin.*

Full weight restoration is an important first step in recovering from anorexia nervosa. But almost always there is more work to do. Often the eating disorder thoughts have become deeply entrenched in the brain and the sufferer has lost sight of who they really are. Untangling and separating the real 'me' from Ed can resemble a battle supreme. Even when aware of the illness, letting go of Ed's rules and thought processes can be extremely scary. A trusted recovery guide can help you conquer fears, get in touch with suppressed feelings and gradually rebuild your own identity.

'If I'm not anorexic, then who am I?'

'Every waking moment my thoughts are consumed by food. How much I can eat, when I can eat it.'

'An eating disorder becomes more than just something you do – it becomes an integral part of who you are – your essence. One of the vital roles of treatment is to find the real you buried beneath the layers of the eating disorder and help you emerge and re-engage in life. This can be an enormous challenge for the sufferer who has spent months or years constructing and supporting the walls of protection that the eating disorder appears to provide from the outside world. The dismantling of the walls, as false as they are, is frightening: the sufferer is left exposed, vulnerable and easily hurt until skills such as resilience are acquired and new behaviours develop.'

'An eating disorder is about more than worrying about what food you can eat for your next meal – it becomes embedded in your thoughts and behaviours and becomes an integral part of who you are. The longer you have the illness, the harder it is to work out which thoughts and behaviours belong to Ed and which reflect the true you. If you are taking medication, this can add to the confusion – do I feel this way because I am me, because of my eating disorder, or because of the medication? The thoughts and behaviours of the illness and self become entwined, leading to much misunderstanding and confusion for you and everyone who knows you.'

'When I began getting well, I wondered how I could return and make up ground at school – I hadn't attended a class for two years – or go to a party, or crack a joke. Suddenly the family home, which had been a prison, became a haven.'

'Having anorexia is horrible. You lose everything. I lost all my sport, I lost my freedom, I had to be watched 24/7, and couldn't do anything. When I wasn't in hospital, I was stuck at home, too sick to go to school, and I lost six precious years of my life. I would struggle with my moods and get angry. It would just happen and I would take it out on people. I don't do that any more. I am enjoying being a teenager.'

'Once I lost the feeling of control that restricting gave me I became more anxious about other changes. Like new clothes or even new shampoo. Suddenly I had lost the only sense of security I had, even if it were false, and the only way to feel safe was to keep everything else exactly the same.'

'I wondered if people would like me if I gained weight. A boy at my first school had been fat and he wasn't liked. This bothered me. I wanted to be liked.'

'I wanted my life back. I wanted to be normal, so I began to eat. At the same time I felt angry that I was "giving in". I didn't want to give in to my parents, to the family-based therapy programme, or the children's hospital system, because then they could all say: "See, we made you better, we made you OK," and tick me off their list.'

'I missed out on the social life and fun that children have when aged 12, 13 and 14. If I wasn't in hospital and there was a party, I'd have to miss it anyway as I would need to go home and have my nose tube inserted. Having the tube meant I couldn't have friends come to my home either. I felt alienated and after five years of anorexia I had difficulty relating to kids my own age.'

'I was afraid of having to give up the nasogastric tube. Being anorexic had become the only thing that I was. If not anorexic, what would I be? And if I gave up the tube, how would people know I was suffering anorexia?'

'Even at my dream size I feel uncomfortable with my body. I can't take compliments; if someone says I look pretty, I think they are lying.'

'I was told I was well but I knew I was not. I looked well, my weight was OK to the outside world and people thought I was fine, but I was not well within. The illness is with me all the time. I can function but it is still there. I am physically healthy yet in some ways remain emotionally dead.'

'I felt like I was losing a good and loyal friend. My ED had been with me for so long. I had relied on it to get me through stressful times – and to have to rely on my own resources now was absolutely terrifying. I had far more problems with anxiety once I stopped turning to ED habits for a quick fix.'

'Having anorexia was the only thing I could do that my friends couldn't. I could do it better than them. It made me feel worthy at times when I never felt like I could keep up.'

'I had heard that putting on weight would decrease my levels of anxiety, but it didn't. My anxiety went through the roof like it never had before. I felt completely lost. All my comforting rituals and thought processes had been taken away from me – but there was nothing in their place. And without any way of relieving my anxiety I turned on myself; berating myself for gaining weight, dressing in baggy clothes to hide my disgusting body and cutting myself in an attempt to relieve my mental pain.'

'The more weight I gained, the more afraid of other people I became. I felt that being skinny gave me an advantage over others and protected me from bullying and teasing. But if I gained weight I felt I would lose that protection and I knew I didn't have it in me to stand up for myself. So I hid myself away, just in case.'

'A vital role of treatment, apart from eating three meals and three snacks a day, is to help you regain your sense of self, which may have been suppressed by the eating disorder for months – or years – and to re-engage in life. This can be a terrifying prospect when you have spent a long time trying to get through each day, and handle all forms of anxiety, by counting calories. The eating disorder has become a gear-stick for getting through life. Without its rules, doomed to fail and false as they turn out to be, you don't know how to live "normally", and feel frighteningly exposed and vulnerable. Hard work over a long period is needed to gradually break down the rigidity of the eating disorder, and replace it with coping skills that others take for granted – skills of resilience and tools to increase self-worth and compassion.'

# Survivor story: a breakthrough conversation

## Bulimia nervosa

Sophie Skover is the author of *The Continuous Appetite*, a life coach and an inspirational speaker, who works to help others experience harmony in their lives. She became passionate about this 'life changing' path after healing from bulimia. Sophie has developed The Continuous Appetite programme to help people discover the meaning underneath their food cravings and give them techniques to use when a food craving surfaces, which results in the end to emotional overeating. Sophie's experience is that with the right tools and support you can heal from the effects of bulimia. Today, her outlook on life contrasts with the torment experienced when in the grips of the illness and struggling to embark on recovery. Sophie shares a milestone moment:

**Therapist:** How was your week?

**Sophie:** It was OK.

*It was far from OK, I feel so fat in my body. I have lost weight but still feel fat. I have changed my diet and started eating carbs because that is what everyone tells me to do, so I have done it, but now I feel loose and fat.*

**Therapist:** Did you have any new awareness this week?

**Sophie:** Yes. That I need to stop eating so much to fill in the blanks; I know I should be facing my feelings instead of numbing them with food, but I cannot seem to gain that control.

*Why can't I stop eating so much? Why can't she give me the answer to this? Why is this so hard?*

**Therapist:** I want you to think back to the last time you overate and sit with that picture for a moment.

**Sophie:** OK.

*Easy, it was right before I came here.*

**Therapist:** Next I want you think about what happened that day?

**Sophie:** I was having a bad day because the lecturer made me feel stupid when I asked a question.

*I always feel so bad inside and the fleeting moment I put food in my mouth I feel better, but then it passes so I have to eat more and more. Then I am overridden with guilt so I have to get the food out of me.*

**Therapist:** Now I want you to think about what emotion you were feeling.

**Sophie:** Stupid and worthless.

*Why is she making me feel worse, she is about to get me angry.*

**Therapist:** Next I want you think about what that emotion feels like.

**Sophie:** I don't know.

*I am about to scream. Why is she doing this to me, why is she making me face the most painful parts of myself?*

**Therapist:** You may feel uncomfortable doing this, Sophie, but that is OK. We need to face the monsters in our closet to see that they are really powerless. It is kind of like being in a dark room and feeling around in the dark for the doorknob. Don't panic, just keep searching, because once you find that doorknob you can then open it to see the light. So can you hang in there with me?

**Sophie:** OK.

*Exhale, OK, I can do this. This is the feeling that usually comes right before I binge.*

**Therapist:** So what does that feeling feel like within?

**Sophie:** It is like a panic, a rush that makes me feel like I am going to die and all that I can think about is food.

*OMG, I can't believe I just said that.*

**Therapist:** So you feel panic. Well, want do you want to feel?

**Sophie:** I want to feel like I can handle life and the littlest fluctuations that come with it without bingeing.

*That would be so nice.*

**Therapist:** Sophie, I am so proud of you for admitting that, because now we can work on some tools to get you there.

**Sophie:** People can actually live in that place?

*I hope I can be one of those people one day.*

**Therapist:** Absolutely!

**Sophie:** What do I need to do to get there?

*…inner chatter has stopped, listening has started.*

**Therapist:** Begin facing your emotions; really feel them. It is OK to feel what you feel! And believe in yourself. You can get through this and one day you will be on the other side of this, victorious. Believe this!

**Sophie:** I will try.

*…inner chatter has still stopped.*

**Therapist:** Sophie, remember, you can heal; you can get through this. You will be OK.

# Survivor story: a crossroad moment

The recovery journey for adult sufferers presents many challenges – but as survivors attest, they can be overcome. Letting go of Ed is a frightening process, requiring support from others. This support may require acceptance of a temporary but humiliating loss of independence – like being treated like a child at meal time by parents or partner. Recovery rate may be impeded and relationships may feel strained in the short term. The solution will be different for each person; be open to considering all options as you might be surprised what works for you – and what people are willing to do to support you.

## Anorexia nervosa

When Kelly, who shares her Survivor Story in Chapter 6 (see pp.69–75), was first diagnosed with anorexia, she felt shocked, devastated and ashamed. Although acknowledging that she had issues with food, Kelly had not thought her behaviour might be a mental illness. From a regular suburban family, Kelly had attended good Catholic schools and university, and had travelled. She had good friends, a nice house, a social life and a (relatively) important job in the Department of Justice. However, like most people with anorexia, while Kelly was perfecting the art of hiding what was really going on, she was silently crying out for help: unknowingly debilitated by anxiety and depression, she was over-exercising, using laxatives and eating like a sparrow. Kelly continues her story, two months into her recovery...

> **Therapist:** Kelly, it is important that your recovery is number one priority. What could be more important than your progress towards becoming well?
>
> **Kelly:** Nothing.
>
> *Lucky she doesn't know that on the way to today's appointment I jumped dangerously from a tram, deciding I could run the last few blocks faster.*

*She looks stern. I can tell that today she won't listen to excuses like 'I must leave early, because an unfinished report is sitting on my desk.'*

*Perhaps I can run back to work after the appointment. At least it will put my mind at ease.*

**Therapist:** Kelly, are you listening? You need to eat *more* – challenge yourself further – really commit 100 per cent to the recovery process. Three weeks have passed since you agreed to eat five times a day.

**Kelly:** I really have been trying.

*I want to meet her expectations. I don't understand why I am failing. If only she knew that a silent, tiny part of my psyche is petrified she might leave me.*

**Therapist:** I'm not seeing improvement – a rice cake and two cups of coffee for breakfast, a salad for dinner – you are starving yourself and don't know it.

**Kelly:** You're right – I'll start eating every meal tomorrow – I promise.

*This is the part I don't understand. I start the week eating well but by mid-week my motivation goes into deep decline and food intake is zero by Friday.*

*Can I stop tossing Mum's pre-prepared frozen dinners in the bin, running around the park in the rain, leaving the supermarket empty-handed – no food in the pantry; eating an apple for lunch; dodging invitations to dinner? I have vowed to myself to 'start tomorrow' each day for three weeks – actually it has been years.*

**Therapist:** Have you considered going home to live with your parents for a while?

**Kelly:** No! I can't. What about my job, my house? I can't just pack up and leave! Live with my parents – we would kill each other! I can't go home!

*She says that like it is no big deal – not a life-changing, backward step that signifies the most catastrophic of failures. Of course I haven't thought about living with my parents – why would I? – things aren't that bad. Surely there has to be another way!*

*I agree I need some kind of break, more along the lines of a romance, career change or overseas holiday; but not being shanghaied back to parents.*

*The therapist clearly doesn't understand that I was hardly a model child. I hadn't put a foot wrong in my early years – I was regularly praised for helpfulness, goodness and kindness. But a switch flicked in my teenage years and memories are of temper tantrums, fights and wanting to be alone. I was horrible – can't deny it.*

*I can't go back home, can I?*

**Therapist:** Yes you can, because your family's love and care are integral to your recovery.

## Frequent question: How do I know when 'enough is enough' in helping my child?

*Experienced carer, Veronica Kamerling, provides invaluable, heartfelt advice:*

The experience of having two daughters who developed an eating disorder, both of whom are now in recovery, has led to us becoming a much closer and healthier family unit. This is due in part to me having learnt how to 'let go' and acknowledge where the boundaries are in terms of letting my children take responsibility for their own lives. Because of what I went through and ultimately learnt from, I was determined to try to help other carers who are struggling today as I did when my children were ill. To this end I am now a trainer running carer workshops. I also facilitate a support group. For more information on all that I do go to my website: www.eatingdisordersandcarers.co.uk.

The role of a carer is like the never-ending story. It can go on and on, 24 hours a day, seven days a week. The task of guiding your loved one towards recovery is often lonely, frightening and thankless. Coping with this tortuous test of endurance will be easier if you look after your own needs along the way. Ideally, take regular time out to replenish your energy. Carer support networks, both local and online, can be an invaluable resource – for both emotional help and building up skills for outsmarting Ed. To see a loved one regain their identity and resume a normal lifestyle is a truly special achievement. Often, carers also learn a lot about themselves along the way.

For instance, my daughter's ability to develop and mature was hampered because I wouldn't let go – I would help her find a job, find a flat – my helping was obsessive – anything she said, I would do better – I did not realize it, but she needed to get away from my smothering attitude and take responsibility for her own attitude and actions.

I learnt that as a carer, I had to recognize and be open to accepting that looking after someone with a mental health problem is different to looking after someone with a normal medical illness. Many parents over-smother and I was one of them. We feel like doing everything. But helping a child recover from an ED is about setting and recognizing the boundaries and being open to being told how to do things.

I am a compulsive helper, and had an obsession built out of my own low self-esteem. My relationship with food has been distinctly suspect. It has always been about control. It manifested in being a helper to the world and yet I was to learn it wasn't really about helping – it was about controlling.

To get to where I am now and to be in a position to help my daughter recover was not an overnight fix. I attended carer workshops for three years. The achievement of addressing and building up my self-esteem, as well as helping my daughter, brings rewards to all areas of my life.

## Frequent question: How do I get past that point of 'just doing enough to get by' and gaining full freedom from Ed?

*Authors June Alexander and Shannon Cutts met in Minneapolis at the 2009 annual conference of the National Eating Disorders Association. It was a case of instant rapport and friendship for Shannon, from Texas, and June, from Victoria (Australia). Both had experienced the hard struggle that comes in regaining a full life from an eating disorder and were now sharing their story of recovery to inspire others. Here they combine the wisdom of their experience:*

So you are constantly see-sawing between what you know is right (examples: three meals and three snacks a day, no stepping on scales, attending to feelings as they arise) and the lure of your cosy entrenched ED behaviours that offer a quick but short-lived 'escape' (numbing or suppressing your feelings through bingeing, restricting, over-exercising). You know what you need to do to get to the next level of recovery – to feel free in the long run – but you are not sufficiently motivated to ignore Ed's ever-ready nudge-nudge of immediate gratification. You know that weighing, giving yourself a pinch test ('How far do my hip bones stick out today?'), or walking out the door without breakfast in your tummy is a bad idea because this feeds Ed, but before you know it, you find yourself doing exactly this anyway.

You feel depressed, thinking you will be stuck in this rut forever. You, and everyone around you, suffer from the outfall of self-loathing and mood swings. Frustration is not a strong enough word. You look normal and it's easy to think 'Why not keep doing just enough to get by – just keep going through the motions?', but not following your food plan exactly, and not being totally honest with yourself, your loved ones or your therapist. The thought of pushing yourself to regain more of the real you is totally scary. So you keep living this part-life. Ed controls the other part. The thought of living without Ed is scary, too – what will take Ed's place? Evicting Ed from your life means you will have to change the way you think, and behave. That's massive.

You already have a lot on your plate – children, partner, ageing parents, studies, work, other health issues, friends going through relationship breakups – really, it's easy to continue to 'depend' on Ed to get through all these stressful moments.

To be candid, though, you are actually postponing the task of facing up to the big issues that are holding you back in life, because while they are unresolved, you have a reason to stay with Ed. On good days, when you have clarity, you can see the reality; you can see what you need to do be free, but somehow still don't do it. This bothers you. Even torments you. Should you feel bad about this? Should you force yourself to seek more help, or is it OK to wait until you feel you have more time – until one day you have suddenly 'had enough' of living this way and resolve without hesitation to confront your illness and commit yourself to exploring life without and beyond Ed?

Motivation, like energy levels, ambition and frustration, may wax and wane from day to day. Generally, people recovering from eating disorders tend to be highly perfectionistic, and want to do a good job at whatever they decide to do, so it can be very hard to manage the daily ups and downs, and the waxing and waning of enthusiasm and motivation encountered in the recovery journey.

Sometimes it seems to take a certain amount of suffering and endurance to reach the point where you decide: 'I've had enough,' 'I'm going to fight back,' 'I want my life,' 'I want to find out who I am without the eating disorder bossing me every hour of every day,' 'I want to find out what it is like to be free.'

Let's face it. Ed's dominating and manipulative nature is tough on someone who is conscientious, sensitive and perfectionistic.

> 'Studying is a struggle, as concentration is difficult. I don't like to start anything I cannot confidently excel at. The thought of achieving anything less than 100 per cent is unbearable. If I consider there is any risk I won't attain a perfect score in tests and exams, I prefer not to try at all.'
>
> – *Adolescent girl with anorexia*

When you see life in black and white, it can be hard to learn that grey is not only acceptable, but also necessary. Breaking down the rigid thinking patterns is like chipping away at a hunk of marble with a wooden toothpick. It's hard to break through. But with freedom depending on it, you look around for other tools and acquire patience, self-love, acceptance, self-compassion, self-awareness, mindfulness and maybe an ice pick or two. You learn that every tiny chip is cause for celebration. There is no quick fix – the shift from being a prisoner to being free of Ed is a gradual metamorphosis. Accepting this relieves the pressure to conquer everything in a day.

> 'Every day I strove to make progress, listing my positives in my diary – calling a friend, smiling at a stranger, buying a book for one of my children. I had to get strong enough and sufficiently self-aware to stop my binge impulse. I would beat my torment at its game.'
>
> – *Mother with bulimia*

You may be experiencing something similar.

You may also be setting aside your natural intuition and wisdom which is telling you that, given your full plate with school, family and other things that are going on, you simply don't have enough support to push yourself through some of those comfort zones without terrible risk of relapse. Human babies get the instinct to walk before they are ready, so they fall over, get up and try again; baby birds often fall to the ground on their first several attempts to leave the nest and fly. In the same way, you may be 'crawling' towards the idea of pushing through ED comfort zones by trying ideas on for size, but do not yet feel emotionally, mentally and relationally equipped to really let go, and live your life without Ed.

So be it. Recovery takes the time it takes. Like us, you have to learn that not only is nobody going to take your eating disorder away, but also that nobody else can. Only you can eliminate your eating disorder, and you have to feel strong enough to remove this thing that has been a consistent source of refuge by equipping yourself with positive resources to cope with life.

'My children's dad, having adamantly said "No" to our young daughter living with me, was briefly off my favourite person list. In my mind, my parents – by welcoming him and his new woman, and giving him food for his household – were helping to keep my daughter from me. To numb my feelings, I ate some cookies, about three. That was enough to break my control for the day. I began to weep but rallied and thought: "I must focus on the people who help me feel I'm OK and respect me. I cannot live my life through my children, or anyone else. I must live first and foremost for myself. What a discovery!"'

*– Adult woman with bulimia*

You may not have the resources yet – what are your other coping skills like? If your eating disorder is still the place you turn to for comfort and identity, then first you need to find other, healthier comforts (that may not seem trustworthy at first, but will prove to be far less frightening as you dare to trust them more and more) and you will have to build an identity for yourself that stands free and clear of Ed. In this way, recovery really is like leaving a bad relationship.

You have been with Ed for so long you are no longer certain who you would be if alone. You wonder how you can possibly separate yourself and, if you do, how you can possibly be 'whole' and stand on your own two feet.

'Changing my thought pattern was a challenge. I had to convince myself that there was no need to binge or overeat "today" because I was free to eat when I felt hungry "tomorrow". This was both liberating and frightening. I had to let go of the gear-stick that had been guiding my life since childhood, a gear-stick that had two speeds: bad or good, control or out of control, depending on whether I was bingeing or starving. Knowing that this gear-stick or thought was controlled by my illness was a big step forward. Letting go of the gear-stick was another.

It occupied a huge part of my mind. Replacing it with a safe and secure foundation would not be easy. In free fall, I let my eating disorder go to the winds for eight weeks. Then I hit a snag. Depressed, I thought of quitting my medication and ate myself to sleep. The next morning, feeling hot, wet from anxiety attacks and sick, I resolved to count calories to ease my guilt. Then I remembered that I had the right to eat when hungry, that I must relax and deep breathe, but DON'T COUNT CALORIES. Gradually, the urge to count calories faded right away.'

*– Adult woman with bulimia*

Maybe this is where your work lies. Rather than focusing so hard on barrelling through each of your various comfort zones like a bull in a china shop, beating yourself up more and more each time you fail to charge over the finish line, take a different approach. Be gentle. Ask yourself – very kindly – 'What is holding me back?' 'What would give me the courage to push through just this one comfort zone?' (Whatever you do – don't try to tackle all of them at once as this may set you up for failure.)

When the black and white must-do approach or a big dose of shame and guilt fail to be motivational, try gentleness with yourself. Treat yourself with the same love, care and respect that you shower upon your best friend. Try this approach and see what insights it yields. Very likely, you will start to see that Ed is really not your type at all.

'My happiness always rose when my children came for a visit. One evening, my daughter came for the evening meal and brought a gift: a beautiful wall hanging, which she had designed and made in her garment construction class at school. I hung it on my bedroom wall immediately. That evening, her father came to collect her and stayed for a chat over a cup of coffee. For a moment I was normal.'

*– Mother recovering from anorexia / bulimia*

# Frequent question: How can I support a friend in recovery?

*Shannon Cutts, founder of the first global eating disorders mentoring community, MentorCONNECT (www.mentorconnect-ed.org), and author of* Beating Ana: How to Outsmart Your Eating Disorder and Take Your Life Back, *loves this question as it conjures a picture of a friend surrounded by warm support from someone who loves them very much. Shannon suggests:*

The best way to support a friend in recovery is to first accept that you do not need to understand eating disorders in order to understand suffering. If you have ever suffered from anything so challenging it made you hold your breath and think 'I don't know if I will get through this,' then you already know what your friend is going through each and every day of the healing process.

It is also important to remember that as a friend, your role on the support team is to be a friend. You are not supposed to be a counselor or therapist, a doctor or dietician. You can remind your friend to visit those professionals when support is needed on medical or dietary matters, and this can also be very helpful. Do not let your friend use you as a substitute professional because that is dangerous for you both. But you can listen, you can empathize, you can be a voice of wisdom in reminding your friend of the right thing to do if they need professional support as well as your friendship (which is likely the case).

Another great way to support a friend in recovery is to ask your friend what they need. Maybe they need a person to eat with, someone who can talk and laugh with them so eating isn't as stressful, or someone to walk or play games with afterwards to get their mind off the meal or snack just consumed. But if you don't know what to do, then ask. Asking, at the very least, says 'I care.'

You can also show your support by (if applicable) moderating your own conversation away from food, weight, appearance and other issues that can be stressful to your friend. If you have body image concerns of your own, or you 'feel fat' one day, recognize that your recovering friend is not the right person to share those concerns with, because this will be stressful to hear. So make sure you have your own sources of support in any area where you need it, because at this point, your role in your recovering friend's life will be more focused on you supporting them than the other way around – at least until they get stronger.

Finally, do not cast yourself as their sole source of support. Encourage your friend to reach out, reminding them that if you are able to be there, others likely will be too. The more social support a recovering person has, the stronger they will feel while recovering.

# PART FOUR
Recovery

# 12

## Behaviour

*Don't try to protect me from my mistakes. Let me live them, feel them, hate them and even regret them. Only through turning mistakes into lessons will I learn not to repeat them.*

## Ed doesn't just go away

Recovery means something different to everyone – depending on how far along the track you are in regaining your identity. Full recovery, which can be defined as being free of eating disorder thoughts and behaviours, is the ultimate goal. It is possible at every age. Don't settle for less. Imagine competing in the marathon race at the Olympic Games and pulling out five kilometres from the finish line – because you think that's 'good enough'. Don't settle for a part recovery when, with a bit more effort, you can get over the line, leave Ed behind and reap the rewards of a full recovery. This chapter explores how the voice and language of Ed changes as we progress along the recovery journey. Basically, recovery means 'getting your life back' from the eating disorder, and the meaning of this may differ slightly for each person. Recovery tends to be gradual, with markers of progress along the way. For example, resuming a physical activity – perhaps joining a school sports team or aerobics class – when weight resumes a healthy level, and resuming responsibility for preparing and eating meals. While weight restoration is vital, recovery does not end there. Recovery also involves restoration of normal thinking processes and the brain can take a long time to heal. The restoration of weight is necessary for thought processes to normalize but Ed thoughts can remain loud and clear for some time after the scales say you're 'all better now'.

> 'My life would have been easier on many fronts if I had been made aware my personality was susceptible to anorexia and to anxiety and that I could relapse, and that recovery is not a matter of achieving a certain weight or BMI. The illness is in the mind. Getting well takes much longer and ongoing vigilance.'
>
> *– Adult woman aged 35*

The need for a sense of control can go through a transitional stage while new ways of living are explored:

> 'My daughter remains obsessed with cleanliness and everything is in order in her room. If I move a pin she knows. She is very particular about what she wears and is very organized. She has an inventory of my groceries. Everything is healthy and she checks labels. She knows exactly how many cans of beans and rice we have and she tells me what to do. The fridge is very organized. She knows where everything is. I have returned to work and come home to find my groceries are all in line, in order. Sometimes I feel like kicking the cans. Sometimes I put something in a different place and she gets angry.'
>
> *– Mother of 18-year-old daughter*

Sometimes recovery comprises one step forward and one step back:

 **@husband** You look lovely in that dress.

**@sufferer** Thanks honey ☺ Actually, I agree it doesn't look too bad. My figure is OK.

*The next day…*

**@husband** You look lovely in that dress. The colour really suits you.

**@sufferer** Are you kidding? I look like a hippo. My thighs are so fat; I can see the rolls bulging out everywhere! I cannot leave the house today. I'm changing back into my tracksuit.

**@survivor** Everybody has good days and bad days on the recovery journey. Your loved one may be able to accept the difficult changes that she is making one moment, and unable to accept them the next. Persevere, and gradually the good days will increase.

---

**@friend** You look all back to normal! I'm so glad you're better now – and just in time for the school formal. What do you think you'll wear?

**@teensufferer** *There is no way I'm going to the formal. For one thing, I'd look like an elephant in a sleeveless gown – no one will go with me looking like this, and if they do it's just because they feel sorry for me. I can't believe they all think I'm 'fixed'. What a joke. I'm already feeling anxious.*

**@survivor** In early recovery the Ed voice remains loud; in fact, it may be raging, because Ed feels cornered and threatened. This is a difficult time because many people – including some health professionals – do not understand that weight restoration is only one part of the recovery process. Much inner healing is yet to take place. It is natural to feel anxious and to feel an urge to isolate yourself. Your support network can explain what is happening and help you not only to resist the urge to withdraw but to start planning your dress for the formal. Engaging in enjoyable events like a formal will show Ed that you are determined to live your life and have fun. The more you do this, the weaker and more silent Ed's voice will become. Eventually it will be extinguished and your true self will blossom.

## Ed is sneaky

Constant vigilance is required for people recovering from eating disorders – and one of the most vulnerable times is when recovery is within grasp. Ed likes a free ride and will take any opportunity to sneak back. Any stress or change may trigger a relapse. Eating disorder behaviours are hard to break. The sufferer may yet be convinced that Ed habits have not worked well as a coping tool in the past and these habits or behaviours can click in like a default button when dealing with a difficult or challenging time. Ed will tell any lies it needs to regain compliance and before you know it, Ed's back in the box seat of your mind.

'I wanted to appear I was OK, and not let people down: the people who had supported me for years – I couldn't let them know I wasn't 100 per cent like I was "supposed" to be. But following a series of very stressful events, I picked up my rules of eating again; the same food, at the same time, every day. These thoughts returned quickly. I thought I was quelling my anxiety but I was feeding it. Anorexia is very sneaky. The relapse swooped in within six weeks.'

*– Adult woman*

**@teensufferer** I'm at least three kilograms over what the doctor wants me to be – I only want to lose those three kilograms – surely that's reasonable? Other people are allowed to lose weight and feel good about it – it's not fair that I am made to feel guilty just because I want to lose unnecessary weight.

 **@survivor** Being honest and talking these thoughts out with your healthcare professionals is important. Sometimes your safest weight will be several kilograms above what your doctor originally thought – 'safest' meaning the weight at which the Ed thoughts and behaviours are the quietest. Talking through 'why' you really want to lose the weight is vital as well. It needs to be discussed and resolved to achieve another step on your recovery path.

---

**@sufferer** I'm not 100 per cent sure I can rejoin the gym yet…

**@Ed** *It's cool, you know what you're doing now. You've experienced the over-exercise thing and you know how to control it. You'll be fine. Exercise is really important.*

**@sufferer** No. I need to talk to my
therapist first and come clean about these Ed
thoughts before I sign up.

**@survivor** Separating your healthy, cautious
thoughts from the enticing Ed thoughts is vital
in recovery – as is learning to be truly honest
with your treatment team. Acquiring self-
awareness skills can help a lot here. If your
thoughts encourage you to deny your true self
in sharing with your treatment team take this
as a warning to be alert! To increase your
resilience, write down your thought and that
of your Ed and share with your therapist, and
to yourself whenever you feel a weak moment
coming on. Focus on your thought and delete
the Ed thought. Gradually this difficult task
will become easier.

---

**@sufferer** I know I have to remember
to eat, but it's really hard to break my
old habits.

**@Ed** *You need a really strict routine.
Eat the same things at the same time each day
and then you'll be OK. This will also help you
keep your anxiety under control. Just make
sure you are really strict – if you make a
mistake your anxiety will skyrocket.*

**@sufferer** You're right. I need to keep
a food diary to make sure I'm not forgetting
to do anything – if I make a mistake I feel
terrible and hate myself – sticking to rules is
the only way to keep recovery on track.

**@survivor** Eating disorder thoughts have a sneaky way of adapting, to avoid being noticed. They can disguise themselves as recovery thoughts, making you think they are supporting you, when really they are setting you up for a fall. Forget the food diary and make a conscious effort to vary your foods. Trying to keep your eating habits 'strict' and 'under control' is like a relapse in disguise. Remember that while full recovery is possible, the underlying biological and temperamental predisposition will always be there. Be vigilant with self-care, always ensuring you have good nutrition, maintain a healthy body weight, get plenty of sleep, and enjoy regular exercise. Seek help for any co-morbid mental disorder or physical illness as they can trigger relapse. A low-stress life and being surrounded by supportive people, who know you well, are aware of your eating disorder history, and are prepared to intervene if necessary, is ideal.

---

 **@mum** Right, first things first. Why did you say 'no' to a scone?

**@sufferer** Oh *laughs* I've already eaten, that's all Mum. I promise.

 **@survivor** All sorts of things can trigger a relapse, from a tiny loss of weight to worrying about school or work. Being watchful for signs that a relapse might be starting – such as eliminating a favourite food and then covering up about it – can help to stop a relapse before it gets started. You may believe that you will not relapse because you don't want to relapse, or because you are no longer driven to be thin. Nevertheless, it is possible to relapse unintentionally, without dieting. Some relapses occur as a result of emotional stress or unintentional malnourishment (for example, due to illness, surgery, bereavement). Any food cutback, even the regular date scone shared with your mother or friend at an afternoon catch-up, is potentially a red flag for someone with an eating disorder history.

---

 **@mum** You have a blog! Why didn't you tell me? You shouldn't be talking about your problems on the Internet for strangers to see! Don't be so selfish and self-absorbed – stop hanging your dirty washing out for all to see.

**@youngadultsufferer** My head is exploding with so much talk and non-stop thoughts – I need to get it out. I need to talk, to write, to see my thoughts and to share with others who really understand.

*Why can't she see that this isn't about her? This isn't about seeking attention – it's about needing support.*

 **@survivor** Talking to people with shared experiences can be a really powerful tool for recovery. For some people, group therapy works really well. But more and more people are turning to social media to find supportive friends who can give each other immediate advice on strategies to help with slips, and provide encouragement and understanding when you need it most. Even in the middle of the night, someone is awake on the other side of the world and will respond to a call for help. Social media that draws on evidence-based research and supports full recovery has many benefits for people with eating disorders. While it cannot take the place of professional treatment, it can help overcome the big issue of isolation for both carers and sufferers.

---

 **@doctor** Your weight was stable for a few months, but I notice that it has dropped a bit this time – do you know why this is so?

**@sufferer** I didn't really mean to, but I have to admit I feel better without those extra few kilograms. And I had a little bit of room to lose weight anyway – I was sitting over the minimum weight we had agreed on.

 **@doctor** So do you think you will stay at this weight now?

**@sufferer** No, I'm still a kilogram over that minimum weight, so I'll lose that too. To be totally honest, I was more comfortable a couple of kilograms lower than the minimum weight too – but I won't lose any more than that. Just another one or two, or maybe three kilograms…

**@survivor** For many people, losing one or two kilograms starts and stops at that, but for sufferers of anorexia, such a loss in recovery can allow Ed thoughts and behaviours to sweep back like a tsunami. Many survivors in full recovery say the best weight for their mental, emotional and physical health is a few kilograms more than the recommended weight. The little bit of extra weight seems to act like a buffer or extra insurance against sneaky Ed.

---

**@sufferer** I will go to the mental health treatment centre this Sunday; my psychiatrist has been encouraging my admission for a long time. I realize that if I don't go, I will just be deferring my recovery (again), and that's not what I want. I want to be free.

**@Ed** *But Sunday morning is when your children are having their friends over for a play and they will want you to fix lunch! Surely you want to be home to look after them?*

**@sufferer** Yes! Of course! I'll call and cancel the admission. It is not important. Another day, another day…

 **@survivor** Recovery is a demanding challenge and, for success, must be top priority. The need to 'fit your own oxygen mask before helping others' is imperative. Yes, you want to be a good mother, but taking a little time out now, and really getting well, will mean the difference between struggling to be a good mother despite Ed's torment in the short term and supporting and enjoying your children as your true self, free of nasty Ed, in the long term.

---

**@teensufferer** That was a really challenging session with the therapist. But my GP says when our discussion is uncomfortable it's because we're talking about the right things.

**@mum** I'm really proud of you for persevering. The sessions may be upsetting but they are helping you big time.

**@Ed** *She has to be kidding. Making you upset cannot be a good thing. Surely increasing your anxiety is the opposite of what she's supposed to do? If your mother wasn't wasting so much money each week on your therapy, your sister could have those music lessons she wants – and that's far more important than this waste of time, sitting in a therapist's consulting room.*

**@survivor** Recovery involves a constant challenging of eating disorder thoughts and behaviours. It's hard work, and often painful and scary, like climbing a steep mountain. But oh, the view from the summit makes it all worthwhile!

# I'm a failure

Ed gets up to all sorts of devious tricks. We know this. Perhaps the biggest and most hurtful deception of all is the relentless drip-feed message that you are worthless and undeserving – and life is therefore very scary. Recognition that these negative, debilitating thoughts belong to the illness is an important step on the recovery path. Mindfulness and self-awareness skills, learnt with a trusted therapist or recovery guide, are helpful tools in regaining the real 'you'. Such skills enable you to catch, defuse and replace Ed's negative thoughts with positive affirmations. Acceptance that the negative thoughts belong to a diagnosable illness also helps to foster this self-compassion.

**@sufferer** I'm a chef. That's what I'm trained to be. If I can't do my job successfully AND manage recovery successfully then I'm a failure. I should be able to do both. Plenty of other people are able to do their jobs and manage recovery. Why can't I?

**@therapist** You are not a failure. Working around food and working shifts are both really tough gigs when in recovery. It does not mean you will never be able to work as a chef and be in recovery, but perhaps it does mean you can't do both straight away. Your recovery has to come first. Recover, and you will be amazed at how your choices increase.

**@survivor** Wanting to handle 'everything' is a common trait among people with eating disorders. Learning to pace yourself and put yourself first is vital for successful and ongoing recovery. To take care of others you must first take care of yourself.

**@friend** Why did you wear such tight fitting obvious clothes and flaunt yourself when you were so underweight – and now that you look fantastic, you hide your body? I don't get it!

**@teensufferer** *I knew I was too thin – it made me special. Everyone was impressed and wanted to be like me. It made me feel good. Now I am nothing. I'm just like everyone else. I can't stand it. There's nothing special about me now.*

 **@survivor** It helps to know that mental and emotional recovery typically lags far behind physical recovery. The physical body has to heal first, through full nutrition and abstinence from bingeing and purging, before Ed's voice will start to subside. So stick with it, these feelings of worthlessness and lack of identity are common and will pass. There is much self-discovery to look forward to.

---

 **@mum** Why didn't you tell me you are struggling again? Why didn't you tell me right at the start?

**@adultsufferer** Mum, you have cancer. I'm supposed to be taking care of you this time. You and Dad have taken care of me for so long – I wanted to do this for you without being a burden. Just this once I wanted to do something right.

 **@survivor** Being a carer for someone you love can be one of the biggest stresses there is. But if you're not looking after yourself at the same time then you are doing nobody a

favour. Self-care must come first, to enable
you to care for others. This is particularly true
for people who have recovered or are
recovering from an eating disorder.
Remember that your Ed voice will persist as
long as you are undernourished or bingeing
and purging – and even then you need to
remain vigilant. If you miss a meal and think,
'Oh, I feel less anxious, so I think I will miss
another and I will feel even better,' Ed is
fooling you big time. Once you start to slip, it
is hard to stop. If you realize you have started
to regress, it is better by far to slip only a
short way down the mountain side, than all
the way into a ravine. Be courageous and
true to yourself – reach out for help
immediately. Don't delay. Your loved ones will
understand and so will your therapist. You
need their support.

## Life is beautiful

Recovery may seem unattainable right now. It may appear in the
distance as something 'other people' do. The good news is that
you *can* recover too. First you need to surround yourself with a
safety net of people who have your best interests at heart. Aside
from your treatment team, recovery guides can come from any
walk of life – if you feel safe with them, and trust them enough
to share your story, hang on to them! If your illness has caused
alienation from your family of origin, create a family of choice.
You may have one recovery guide, or multiple recovery guides. The
number does not matter but one is essential. The recovery guide
is a ready anchor whenever Ed creates a storm. Family, friends
(both in real life and online), researchers, healthcare professionals,
priests, rabbis, even your local hairdresser or dentist can be part
of your support network for recovery. Share with these people
and let them look out for you; dare to believe them when you
feel too anxious or confused to believe in yourself. Generally, the

more people who understand and support the challenge you are taking on, the better. Recovery guides or mentors have your best interests at heart. They will toss you a lifeline when you feel you are drowning in a sea of Ed. They will be there to catch you when you slip and fall; they will be beside you all the way and lead you to safety. They won't judge you; they will quietly and patiently encourage you to recognize and let go of the Ed thoughts and behaviours and rediscover the real YOU. They will help you see that it is OK to avoid people and situations that trigger anxiety and a loss of confidence. They will provide a ring of support when you feel ready to challenge obstacles that are impeding your progress. They are prepared to do all this because they believe in you. All you need to do is trust them. Recovery is worth your effort.

 **@dad** We were delighted when, without prompting, our daughter began to describe something that had happened at school. For months she had shared nothing. Slowly, our daughter's personality began to shine through. At first, her illness would interrupt after a few words and shut us out, but gradually there was more of our daughter and less anorexia. It was a big moment when she came home from school and shared an entire joke she had heard that day.

 **@survivor** Ed doesn't like you to be happy, or to socialize with others. It wants to isolate and silence you. To share a full joke in the early stage of recovery is a big achievement; it is evidence that recovery is definitely happening.

**@mum** Your doctor and I have agreed that your weight is now acceptable and stable enough for you to start playing your sport again.

**@teensufferer** Fantastic!

 **@mum** But remember, this is a privilege. If you lose weight, or I can see your Ed habits creeping back in then the sport will need to stop again. This is for your own safety.

**@teensufferer** Yep, I get it.

 **@survivor** Being allowed to resume something you love can make you feel more like your true self. You suddenly see 'possibilities', a glimpse of life beyond the eating disorder. Having something good happen can boost your resilience and determination to ignore the Ed voice. If the thought of good health does not inspire you to go to the next level on the recovery path, perhaps the chance to play a sport you love, or enrol for some study that really interests you, will spur you on.

# 13

---

# Food

---

*Fear about food is a wall of nothing through which you can pass.*

Throughout the illness you may have been told an eating disorder is 'not about the food'. Which is true in a way – because it is about much *more* than food. Because you are eating three meals and three snacks a day, and weight is restored, does not mean you are 'well'. Recovery takes time. But throughout recovery and beyond, food retains a central focus: it is the stick with which the illness beats us and yet we need to eat it. The habits, rituals and feeling that starving or bingeing can provide give temporary and tenuous relief from the anxiety. Turning away from these comforters and resuming normal eating patterns involves not only the breaking of these habits from a practical level, but also coping without the perceived security they provide on an emotional level. Finding a new way of coping with feelings can be scary. It helps to remember that Ed behaviours appease your Ed voice temporarily but strengthen it over time, whereas healthy behaviours may cause your Ed voice to flare up initially, but over time, will pacify and silence the voice. Ed does all it can to make recovery hard work: it gets more aggressive during the refeeding phase and kicks up while you strive to adjust to healthy eating habits and healthy body weight. Being aware of this puts you one step ahead.

The goal in early recovery is to live with the Ed voice but not act on it. This is a tough assignment and guidance from your support team is crucial to help you to withstand Ed's powerful pull. Ignore the pull, and the Ed voice will dissipate over time.

Your best defence is a steady combination of good nutrition, good therapy and excellent self-care. In other words, pamper yourself. You deserve it. Full recovery is achieved and the battle won when Ed's voice is silent.

> 'Finally, senior year came around and college applications started. School was boring and my eating disorder was now threatening to hold me back from going to college. I decided, no way! No way was I going to let this thing keep me from my entire future. So I actually made an effort. Whereas before it had honestly been more important to me to look good than to be healthy, now I NEEDED, with every fibre of my being, to be healthy so my parents would allow me to go to college. I gradually became more stable and by spring was holding my weight steady. I gradually began to eat off the meal plan that I had been on for four years. At first it made me extremely anxious to do so, but after a while it was almost natural. I could eat – just like everyone else ☺'
>
> *– Young adult woman*

## Taking care of business

Ed is smart but you can be smarter. You can develop strategies. Prior preparation and planning can help you to resume normal eating habits and ignore Ed's persistent nagging 'listen to me, listen to me'.

**@middleagedsufferer** I'm going to ask my friends to choose off the menu for me if I find it too challenging.

**@Ed** *You are now officially too hopeless to qualify as a grown-up! What are you, a kid who doesn't know their own mind?*

**@middleagedsufferer** I'm taking care of myself by getting my caring friends to help me and relieve me of this pressure and anxiety. This is my strategy to prevent Ed's voice making me anxious.

**@Ed** *No, this is you making sure that you aren't to blame when you pick the fattest thing on the menu – you just don't want to feel guilty for being a pig.*

**@middleagedsufferer** La, la, la – I'm not listening to you!

---

**@adultfriend** I can't believe you are STILL taking your daughter's lunch to her at school! Don't you think you're taking this 'over-controlling mother' thing a bit far? She's fine now – look at her!

**@mum** I agree she looks fine, and I know she's doing really well. But I also know how quickly this can change and neither of us wants that. I will keep taking lunch to school until my daughter is confident she can handle lunchtime on her own.

**@experiencedcarer** People make comments based on their lack of understanding of eating disorders – sometimes no matter how often you try to educate them. But this is a time where you and your family need to come first. Some friendships may need to go on the shelf for a while.

## Not helpful

Beware: there are plenty of comments out there that are *not* helpful when you are determinedly trying to eat your three meals and three snacks daily. Comments said with good intention, but out of ignorance, can provide fuel for bossy Ed.

 **@friend** I'm so proud of you for eating everything off the plate! Honestly, I don't think I could have eaten more than that! That was like a whole day's worth of calories for me, right there. Great job!

**@Ed** *She's saying what a pig you are – she can't get over how much you just scoffed down. You are revolting.*

**@teensufferer** *I can't believe I ate more than her – her body frame is so much bigger than mine! I ate my usual portion but now I am worried that I ate way too much. I'm such a piggy.*

 **@experiencedcarer** Avoid making comparisons (good or bad) about what someone in recovery is eating. Food intake may vary during recovery and even the smallest increase is often associated with a high level of anxiety.

---

 **@motherinlaw** Why don't we order the same thing – that way you won't be worried about whether I've chosen something 'safer' than you?

**@sufferer** Thank you! That's a great idea.

 **@motherinlaw** OK, let's choose egg salad rolls.

**@sufferer** Sounds good to me.

*Ten minutes later...*

 **@motherinlaw** Oh, that's it, I'm feeling full – I can't eat another bite! That filled up the gap, plus I ate that huge breakfast.

**@Ed** *It's a test! She's trying to see just how much she can beat you by. If you keep eating then she knows she is better than you and has more self-control than you.*

**@sufferer** *So, am I supposed to stop eating now too? The trouble is, I don't know if I am full or not. My hunger and satiety cues have not kicked in yet.*

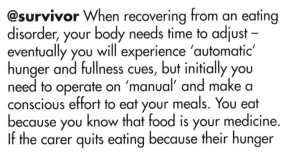 **@survivor** When recovering from an eating disorder, your body needs time to adjust – eventually you will experience 'automatic' hunger and fullness cues, but initially you need to operate on 'manual' and make a conscious effort to eat your meals. You eat because you know that food is your medicine. If the carer quits eating because their hunger

is satiated, doubt may sweep in; you automatically think you should quit eating too – to eat any more, even though you feel like you could and should, may make you feel uncertain and guilty. The carer needs to be aware of the impact of their eating behaviour on the person with the Ed – the carer role is to offer support while you eat your meal (your medicine) and lead by example.

---

 **@partner** It was your idea to go out for lunch – why are you sulking? What is the problem now?

**@youngadultsufferer** *I started getting nervous on the drive here – I should have said something earlier. I want to be here, but I'm starting to panic. I thought I could handle this – but I can't if he rushes me and gets grumpy with me.*

 **@survivor** Don't be afraid or ashamed to speak up and ask for what you need. Explain that your quietness is due to an internal dialogue with Ed. Your partner is not a mind reader – and the more fears you share with him the more he will understand and help you to predict and divert a situation that might cause distress. Many mental and emotional symptoms, including the Ed voice, are caused or exacerbated by a lack of nutrition or chaotic nutrition, and will abate naturally when good nourishment takes place over a number of months. A solution is to invite your partner to assist with the plan – three meals and three snacks a day. Fight the urge to be silent and share your concern about what might be on the lunch menu – allow your partner the opportunity to be supportive.

# 14

## Relationships

*A true life partner is someone whose eyes are open
to all of your faults and loves you anyway.*

As you work your way towards recovery, you will discover your own identity emerging; one with insight, strength, confidence and yes, opinions! But some days are better than others. Some days still feel like rollercoaster days with highs and lows. The mood swings can impact on relationships, causing people around you to feel confused, not knowing what to expect next. Communication with family, partners and friends throughout the recovery journey is vital to keep these relationships alive, honest and fair. Every member of the family and friendship circle has been affected by the eating disorder, so everyone has some adjusting to do. Stick with it and know that the rollercoaster days will subside as obstacles are dealt with and pushed aside.

 **@brother** My relationship with my sister suffered. We had got along really well before the illness struck and then the sister I knew disappeared. As she was in hospital for long periods for four years in a row, we grew distant and our relationship completely changed. Her illness robbed her of her teenage years, and robbed me of a sibling, pretty much. She was fun loving and very happy before the illness, and while she was sick I could see her complete and utter despair, struggling against a big barrier and throwing huge tantrums at her worst. By the time she got well, I had departed home for college. Now we are living in the same city, we are speaking more, but I still feel I don't know her that well.

---

 **@dad** At first, I felt angry and had difficulty divorcing the illness from my child. I still do. Everything seems to centre on her in her mind. This can make her seem incredibly selfish and unable to see other points of view, and she seems unable to acknowledge efforts others are putting in. But I can now see that this is the illness and not her. Looking at it this way makes it easier.

---

 **@husband** For a long while after my wife got better, it was me who felt tired and down. I felt like an elastic band that had been stretched to the limit and was now prone to snapping easily. I had much less patience, and became angrier more quickly. Really, I needed something to help me to get back to my old self, but there was nothing. It was like, OK, my wife is better, and so everything is fine. I suppose I felt a bit numb by the whole experience, and needed re-energizing somehow.

---

**@sufferer** I have different sets of friends. I have my 'eating disorder' friends and my 'normal' friends. My normal friends don't understand how upsetting it can be not to fit into your jeans – they just don't get why I would cry for 20 minutes over that. But I've found it's really important to have those friends who don't 'get it'. They give me a chance to be the old me again. They are helping me to catch up on all the things we used to talk about – and my eating disorder just never comes up. I need both groups really.

## I miss the old me

Learning to love the new recovered 'you' can be trying at times. Ed has bellowed in your mind for months or years, to the point where you hardly know who you are without 'the voice'. It takes time to fill the void. For a start, recovery requires acceptance of a body that looks normal to others but seems foreign to you. A mind still tortured by body-image distress can hamper the adjustment process, and the pull to return to your old body size can seem inviting. You may idealize what life was like back in the grip of your eating disorder. You may feel tempted to go there. But beware, and don't be fooled: this is Ed being sneaky again.

**@husband** I got the photos developed from our trip and they look great. Here, take a look.

**@sufferer** *gasp*

**@husband** What's wrong *now*?

**@sufferer** I look disgusting! Look at how fat I am. I don't deserve to smile. Look at my fat cheeks. I feel horrible now. I don't want to look like that. I feel so ashamed.

**@experiencedcarer** Focus on the fun you had on your holiday. Don't let your weight restoration efforts spoil it. The photos show a happy you – your eyes are twinkling because you are living in the moment. Ed has taken a back seat. See how much you are smiling in the photos – this is the real you shining through. This is what matters. Hit the delete button on the Ed thoughts and start planning your next trip. It is a wonderful gift to have something to look forward to and you deserve it.

## Constant vigilance

Slips and relapses are a reality. They happen; sometimes they happen again and again. Picking yourself up and using what you have learned to strengthen your budding sense of self is far more empowering than berating yourself, and dwelling on the fact that it happened. Support people are a vital resource in keeping a watchful eye for relapse triggers and behaviour.

**@husband** You look a bit tired so I will cook dinner for us tonight. What would you like?

**@sufferer** Whatever you want. I am not hungry. I've had a lot of trouble at work today and I don't feel well.

**@husband** Put your feet up and I'll get you a cup of tea while I prepare our meal. We can then relax together quietly and eat.

 **@survivor** Constant vigilance is necessary both during and after eating disorder treatment. Outside pressures can be a potent trigger for a relapse; any mention of not wanting to eat due to stress – or any other reason – should be a red flag to a watchful carer. Going without a meal won't help solve the crisis at work but it will make you more susceptible to anxiety. Just as people with Diabetes Type 1 need regular injections of insulin to maintain their health, people with eating disorders need regular meals to maintain their health. This is non-negotiable.

---

 **@bigsister** I see the way you look at your friend. Your body shape is not meant to be thin like her. She is a totally different body type. Her gene pool is different. She is taller and has longer limbs – you were not healthy when you were as thin as her.

**@sufferer** Listen, I know that, I had a problem and now I don't. I'm fine now.

*Secretly I still yearn to be as thin as my friend. Why can't I be as thin as her? It's not fair. Why is she allowed to be thin and wear those beautiful clothes like she has just stepped out of a glossy magazine, and I have to be so fat? I hate being this fat!*

**@survivor** Eating disorder recovery is made more difficult by the socio-cultural obsession that you must be thin to be beautiful and successful. Temptation is everywhere and Ed feeds on it. Trust your instincts. If you observe that your loved one is slipping and they are unable to acknowledge this, then this is a warning sign that the Ed thoughts may be creeping in again. Step up vigilance at meal times and share your concern with other members of your support network.

## Recovery takes time

Everyone gets impatient at the length of time recovery takes. It's a long haul for both the carers and the person with the eating disorder. Understanding that this will be a long road from the outset is helpful, but even so, patience is tested in ways you have never thought possible.

 **@mum** I feel very disappointed when I hear that all you do is go to Starbucks and yoga while other people are working hard.

**@Ed** *She's thinks you are so pathetic – you are wasting your life. You need me to make you strong and productive again. The more you fight me the lazier and more hopeless you get!*

**@sufferer** I am in the early stages of recovery and going to Starbucks and drinking a mocha without worrying too much about the calories or going to yoga, instead of running on the treadmill for hours, are a *huge* deal for me. Recovery is hard work! I know you can't see it but I am still actively fighting inner turmoil every day. And it's exhausting.

**@survivor** An eating disorder is a biologically based mental illness. Recovery takes time. Going back to work can be a financially important and healthy step, but needs to occur when the patient and the treatment team agree the time is right.

---

 **@sister** I'll have the pizza, please.

**@adultsufferer** I'll have a side order of green beans, thanks.

 **@sister** Green beans? Seriously, green beans? That's all you're going to eat? Honestly, you are no fun to be around. I thought you were recovered?

**@adultsufferer** Please try to understand. I don't care what you order. I like being here with you – but eating in public is still really challenging for me. Green beans are better than nothing and this is the best I can do for now. I will improve! Let's focus on the fact that I'm here – let's enjoy each other's company, talk about boys, and forget about the food ☺

 **@survivor** Knowing when to express concern at your loved one's eating behaviour is a difficult call during recovery. Realistically, green beans are not adequate for a balanced meal, but on the other hand, progress is being achieved in eating in public. If meat and potato are ordered with the beans on the next outing, the signs will be positive that all will be well. If the beans are the only order the second time, it may be time to challenge the eating disorder afresh.

---

**@friend** Why don't you order something to eat? Aren't you hungry?

**@Ed** *You can't eat in front of her. Anything you order will confirm why you are now so fat. She'll tell everyone how much you ate. They'll all laugh at you.*

**@sufferer** No. I brought something to eat from home and I ate it earlier.

*I wish I could eat as easily as you do. I want so much to be normal, but I'm just not there yet. I am hungry but fear you will judge me and not like me if I eat.*

**@survivor** The person with the eating disorder is possibly telling the truth. But if food is avoided next time you catch up, take this as a warning sign. Gently ask if something is causing concern, avoid making judgemental comments, and seek advice from your support network. Pouncing on and dispelling Ed behaviours as soon as possible is important. The longer the Ed thoughts and behaviours go unheeded, the harder they are to arrest and eradicate.

# 15

## Sense of Self

*What is normal to one person may be
bizarre to another. And that's ok.*

Recovery from an eating disorder is very much a time of discovery
of who we are – like a baby who learns to roll over, crawl, stand
and walk before they run, a person cutting loose from Ed goes
through many stages too. Sometimes, like the baby, we fall over,
we get frustrated, sometimes we may hurt ourselves; but also like
the baby, we find to our joy that perseverance brings freedom.

'It does not have to be a big event that brings you
undone. Sometimes it is the small things. When overtired,
overstressed or overwhelmed the eating disorder thoughts
can creep in. When there is a stressful period – or a very
happy period – it's easy to get caught up in the moment,
and let basic things go, like a snack, and the anorexia can
creep back. It distracts us from ourselves and this is how it
can sneak in while we are focusing on helping others. We
have to look after ourselves first.'

'When I returned to school, a close friend's dad died
suddenly. I realized I had been as upset over eating
a piece of lettuce as this boy was at losing his father. I
was horrified. The trauma and grief in fighting an eating
disorder is immense. Far more than I ever expected or
understood while I was caught up in it.'

'Learning to accept spontaneity and change is the hardest thing! I'd like to be the sort of person who can cope with a sudden decision to go out for a meal after work. Oh, but this is scary.'

'I'm restarting friendships I enjoyed before anorexia intervened, but I still maintain relationships with friends I met during therapy "who have been there". Having friends makes me feel part of the wide world again. Like I exist again.'

'I cannot let Mum and Dad hug me but I can hug girlfriends. With my parents I am still quite angry and I feel like this is my space and "You have done this, and I still hold you responsible for me putting weight on." I don't want them to touch me and feel how much weight I have gained – even the thought makes me feel anxious.'

'Another wonderful gift that recovery is giving me is the ability to really be present with my children. I can sit and watch them play and not be thinking about all the thousands of other little details my mind would normally scream at me. I feel peaceful and forget about everything else.'

'Anorexia is an illness and therefore is separate but it is also mental and is part of you. When you are coming out of it, it is like losing part of yourself. It is a real conundrum. Sometimes the illness will dominate, and you have bad days or weeks.'

'At first I felt hugely anxious at the depth of the void left by my illness. It filled gradually and I don't know how full it is normally but I am happy. It feels full in certain circumstances – like going to movies and watching friends laugh and cry, and helping nieces and nephews build sandcastles at the beach. I love to see people close to me in touch with their feelings.'

'I feel I still almost have a shadow. It is not very tangible but the threat remains. I have relapsed several times.'

'When sick with anorexia I wasn't with my friends, I wasn't going to parties; I wasn't getting my period like other girls. I still feel like I don't belong. I am intimidated easily. I either click with people or don't. I am very reserved at first and then later they say I am "cool". A lot of adults say I am mature. So, I am getting there.'

'Getting well doesn't mean getting fat. Doctors kind of drill this into your head. They say: "We will put a tube in and you will be better" which translates to "We will get you fat and you will be well." The real meaning of "getting well" means regaining your life, waking up and not having to think "I will eat this many calories" and "do this many sit-ups". It means being able to hang out with your friends, or go shopping, and feeling like you belong.'

'For more than a decade, after moving to the city for work and better treatment support, my closest new friends and colleagues knew nothing of my illnesses, anorexia and bulimia. In their eyes, I was normal and I tried to connect and blend even though I always felt on the periphery. I wanted to be treated as normal, because I had children to care for, too. Sometimes, at dinner functions and social events, those who were more observant nudged and said: "Are you feeling OK, is that all you are eating?" but I was an expert in pretending less is more. If people knew about my illness, they would be more inclined to label me. I needed the "cover" of normality until I felt strong enough and resilient enough to "come out" and share my story.'

'My biggest challenge has been coming to terms with the weight coming on, and not being skinny. Sometimes I'm tempted to go back to being skinny as I tend to forget the bad times and have to remind myself of them. Things like having visits and even phone calls restricted. I guess that is why I had so many relapses; my illness was drawing me back and helping me think of new tricks.'

'I find that mindfulness particularly helps me in times of angst, in times where I am about to engage in unhelpful or self-harming behaviours or at times when I am feeling out of control. The non-judgemental, present-centred awareness allows me to think and feel and experience a range of sensations, acknowledge these, accept them and ultimately get on with what I was doing prior to the thought. I no longer have to fuse with these negative thoughts and allow them to affect my every waking hour. Obviously, there are occasions when I struggle, when I find it difficult to allow myself to practise mindfulness, however if I can stop myself before feelings and emotions intensify, I am often able to avoid harmful behaviours.'

'Once I was well I was able to articulate the "benefits" of my anorexia. Nothing derails and undermines women faster than being told they are fat. Frequently, serious women with serious things to say are not taken seriously because of their appearance. I was so insecure that I can now see I was protecting myself from this. Nobody could use that as a reason to undermine me. I felt stronger because, regardless of their talents and abilities, I would always have the one thing that they couldn't achieve – the lowest weight. But weight loss should not be an achievement. Our society has it totally wrong. And I needed to learn skills of self-esteem to realize this.'

'For the first time today I found myself looking at my old clothes wishing I had something a little dressier to wear. Suddenly all my baggy "hiding" clothes didn't suit me any more. I wanted to look nice – and not to impress anyone, but because I have regained my sense of self-respect. I want to look nice for me.'

'Having kids has helped me move on from my eating disorder. My kids have taught me to be more human, not a super impersonator of someone who is perfect – the person always keeping the balls up in the air – as kids are messy, get sick, don't use their manners (at the times when you most want them to) and state their opinions out loud.'

'Some of my closest "new" friends know nothing of my past. Mostly they are other mothers and neighbours that I have met during the course of my children attending kindergarten and school. While I tell myself that there hasn't been much of an opportunity to confide, the truth is that I cherish being perceived as "normal", as after ten years of recovery from anorexia, I still fear being instantly redefined in others' eyes; that I will be watched more closely at a party (I still struggle to eat in the smallest of crowds), greater meaning will be extracted from what I say, or comments will be made if my jeans are hanging loosely or if I refuse a piece of cake. My biggest fear is that all I have achieved could be taken away; that the anorexic voice that tormented me day and night for more than half my lifetime will manage to convince me again that I don't deserve such happiness. But I know I do.'

'Meeting other people suffering the same type of illness has helped me realize that I am not on my own; and I am not bizarre. The understanding that flows from one person with an ED to another – you can't put a price on this.'

'Grandkids have taught me to connect with the kid in me. Being impromptu, living in the moment, being flexible. It's OK to leave that basket of ironing until later and go kick the ball in the park. In fact, don't bother with the ironing at all.'

## Survivor story: understanding the eating disorder 'Voice'

*June Alexander, author of the memoir* A Girl Called Tim — Escape from an Eating Disorder Hell, *reflects on the impact of her eating disorder's mind games:*

I remain amazed and enthralled and horrified at the ability of an eating disorder to twist and turn words. Not only the spoken word but also the silent words that for decades raced incessantly, like champion dodgem cars, around in my mind.

Say one word and my resident eating disorder would grab and magnify it to the point where confusion reigned and common sense was vanquished. One word could trigger a thousand irrational thoughts.

An outsider would never dream of the connection. They would scratch their head, wondering what they had said, as a cloud swept over my face, my sunny nature swallowed up by the eating disorder. Babbling one moment, silent the next.

Family called me 'pig-headed', 'unsociable' and 'stuck up'. This must be how I appeared to them, but inside I was scared, sensitive to criticism and unsure of myself.

I had lived with an eating disorder since age 11 and had no idea what life could be like without the Voice. Frankly, I did not know life could be any other way. By the time I entered adolescence, the language of the eating disorder had become embedded in my thoughts and behaviours; I did not know that my friends did not have a bossy voice in their brain like me.

My mother, who took great pride in home cooking, did not understand what had happened to me. She growled and criticized when I did not eat meals, and when I refused to stop running. Because we did not understand each other, a rift grew between us. I kept to myself, more and more. As I grew into adulthood, the weather became the only safe subject on which to communicate.

From my early twenties onwards, I became aware I was often making decisions that were not in my best interests, and could not understand why.

The Voice did not relate only to food and exercise. It related to relationships. And to feeling safe, stable and secure. Language and communication on every level was affected.

Life was a rollercoaster and I had no idea how to get off. It was scary because chaos was a great partner for my eating disorder. Together the two fouled up both inner and outer translation.

I was in and out of relationships that were attracted to the eating disorder characteristics rather than mine. My doctor kindly labelled the unsuitable relationships as 'mistakes'. The challenge was to turn these mistakes into a lesson. For a long time, I kept going back to be hurt again. For years I could not escape the bullying voice of the eating disorder.

Each time I managed to get on the verge of a safe place – a place where I could be secure and have plenty of support while recovering my 'voice' – I would take fright and make life doubly difficult. Chaos was something I knew about; I yearned for peace within but was scared of it: afraid of the stillness, of the 'nothing' but me and 'it'.

So I would return to a relationship that my treatment team, children and friends had encouraged me for months to leave. I would be aware I was not behaving in my best interests; that I was letting my children down (again); that I was hurting the feelings of a nice man who deep down I knew would be 'safe' and who declared love for me despite my illness; that I was making life really hard for myself – but I would go headlong into fresh chaos and do it anyway.

An eating disorder and communication breakdown; they went together like a horse and carriage.

I would sell a house and go into new debt. One time I even bought a house back that I had sold only three years before – paying almost double, but telling myself I needed to buy this house back, to fix up a mistake in the past. And then my road to peace would become clear; so fuddled was my thinking. The eating disorder had a grand time playing with thoughts and emotions. 'Isolate and destroy' seemed to be its motto.

Emotions? What were they? I had no idea! I reacted to them but did not know how to engage with them.

Eating disorders had been bossing me around since childhood. Now I was a middle-aged woman! Emotions and feelings were a foreign language. I was completely out of touch with both. Besides not knowing how to communicate with others, I had no idea how to communicate with myself.

Then, at age 47, I discovered feelings were the key to beating the horrid eating disorder.

The moment of enlightenment occurred when my therapist suggested identifying the voice of the eating disorder and separating it from the thoughts that belonged to the real me. I could identify the eating disorder language – dominating and manipulative as it was – but catching and defusing it before those dodgem car thoughts roared out of the pits of my brain was a huge challenge.

'Focus on your feelings and food will take care of itself,' my therapist said. She was right. The process took eight years but the day came when I could eat normally, peace reigned in my heart, I stopped moving house just to 'have a new start', I embraced stability, security and safety, I became my own best friend. I rediscovered the voice of self that had been sabotaged by anorexia more than 40 years before. I learnt how to communicate with others and myself.

No more dodgem car thoughts racing around in my head. No more misinterpretation, no more chaos. Everyone who loved me heaved a huge sigh of relief. But none sighed louder than me.

# PART FIVE
# From Recovery to Recovered

# 16

## Aim for a Full Life – You Deserve It

Whether you are 16 or 60, the strength and willpower required to break free from an eating disorder is immense. The first step is to reach out for help without delay. As in preparing for and attempting any great challenge in life, a support team is essential. We hope that your family is there to support you but if not, a family of choice can be created from a trusted friend or friends. One special person who you feel you can trust can make all the difference. Your family, whatever its composition, will be integral to your recovery.

Recovery is complex. First, there is your physical self, requiring a regular and balanced eating pattern. Regaining adequate nourishment for your body is always top priority. You don't expect your car to run without fuel, and you can't run without fuel, either. This essential 'medicine' of three meals and three snacks a day is as vital in maintenance as in recovery. Many survivors find that being a few kilograms over the 'ideal weight' helps provide a buffer and alleviates feelings of anxiety that can drive eating disorder behaviours. Second, there is your psychological self. Acquiring skills will help you to cope with life and its resulting emotions without depending on your eating disorder. Exploring, addressing and resolving any underlying emotional problem can help avoid anxiety build up. Development of self-awareness and mindfulness will help prevent eating disorder thoughts from sabotaging your progress. When you become aware of feeling lost or alone, anxious or vulnerable, be brave, reach out immediately and allow your support team to guide you. This cannot be said enough. Dealing with problems immediately reduces the risk of eating disorder thoughts creeping in.

Setbacks are common but recovery is achievable. Moreover, the temperament and personality traits that create a vulnerability to developing anorexia nervosa, for instance, also have a positive aspect. These traits include attention to detail, concern about consequences and a drive to accomplish and succeed. Take heart from knowing that many people who recover from eating disorders proceed to do very well in life.

There is no 'one road' to the regaining of your self. Every story of recovery has many pathways, depending on many factors. Importantly, we can learn from the experiences of others and avoid pitfalls. Read the inspiring stories of recovery in this chapter and the next three chapters.

# The recovery guide versus the Ed 'voice'
## A message for sufferers

An eating disorder is not a choice. It is a coping tool of sorts, often borne unconsciously out of anxiety to help us feel less stressed about things that we perceive are beyond our control – sadly, it is a tool that is self-destructive. When we are very sick – when Ed has swamped our very being and medical intervention is required – our survival depends on others. People who care about us must fight our illness for us when we are incapable. But as survival turns to recovery, we come to the point where we face a choice. That moment of reckoning, of great clarity, requires us to face a cliff-edge decision: to succumb to Ed's voice, or to fight it. This is the turning point, deciding whether to 'let go of this tiny thread of me, and die'; or 'hold on to this tiny thread and strive to strengthen it and rebuild me'. The following story of recovery illustrates the empowering role of the recovery guide and the internal dialogue that takes place as our true voice fights and develops self-will to overcome the illness voice.

## Pooky Knightsmith

*As soon as Pooky Knightsmith heard about this book, she was keen to share her story because she can vividly remember a time when the Ed voice completely controlled her life. At the time it felt like there was no escape. Pooky hopes that people who are still prisoner to their ED will find hope in her story because she won. She is still beating the voice every day and is using everything she learnt during her illness to help others with eating disorders. Her first book on eating disorders is about to be published, she is a trustee for Beat, the world's largest eating disorder charity, and will complete a PhD on eating disorders next year. The achievement of which Pooky is most proud is that she has found happiness: 'Nothing gives me greater pleasure these days than just being me –surrounded by my loving family and looking forward to a long and happy future with them. Good luck in your battles – you can win too!'*

I suppose that more than anything I felt alone. I used to be surrounded by people who cared, who loved me and only wanted the best for me, but I pushed them away because they cared too much and they wanted to make me fat to keep me 'healthy'. I did the only thing I knew how and I ran away.

I found myself in a university city, supposedly studying for a degree in psychology but actually spending my time studying food packets and poring over recipes I would never make. The 'Voice' constantly reminded me that I didn't deserve to be here. I had flunked my exams but my tutor had taken pity and let me in anyway. And now I was drowning. None of it made sense. However many hours I spent studying, nothing went in. I blindly copied hundreds of pages out of text books, desperate to make sense of it all, the whole time thinking guiltily about the stick of celery I'd eaten hours earlier and feeling disappointed in myself because I'd only lost half a pound since yesterday morning.

I was slowly starving myself to death and no one cared. I'd lost a lot of weight since starting university and the Voice was proud with my progress and urged me to continue. I couldn't write the essays that my tutors demanded but I could deprive myself of food. I didn't deserve to eat anyway. The Voice made sure to remind me of that if ever I wavered.

Nothing could make me question the Voice, until one day a friend broke through. I had known her just a few weeks and I'd made her ANGRY. She took my frail shoulders in her strong rower's hands and physically shook me. Bringing her face level with mine, in a matter-of-fact way she said: 'Everyone is worried about you.' She said: 'It is clear that if you kept on going the way you are, you will be dead. It is very unfair of you to make your new friends watch this happen.' She said I needed to either decide to live, and they'd support me, or die quietly somewhere else.

'Die!' the Voice said – pleased that someone had finally recognized how far we'd come. It was a tempting offer and felt like the ultimate prize. But there was a tiny part of me that began to question the Voice. Someone cared. Maybe I wasn't alone after all?

Despite protestations from the Voice, I decided to try being normal for a while. I even ventured into my college's dining hall for the first time. I rapidly gained weight and was disgusted by my rolls of fat. The Voice constantly taunted me, making every bite I took taste fetid and every pound I gained feel like the end of the world, but I battled on. I knew I could lose it all again if I decided I didn't like being normal after all. I found myself able to understand lectures and I even turned out some half decent essays. I started going out with friends occasionally and to all intents and purposes I really was 'normal'. I wasn't sure I liked it though. The Voice wouldn't go away and I felt out of control of my weight, which seemed to be increasing at a rapid rate.

The Voice was constantly tempting me to return to the safe world of starvation and I was on the brink of caving in when I met Tom. Ten years later, Tom is my husband and father of my two beautiful children, but back then he can't have known quite what he was getting himself into. He chatted me up in my college bar, something I was rather unaccustomed to, and took a real interest in me. I was convinced he would instantly forget me, but within 24 hours he took me for coffee and within a week we were considered a couple.

I could talk to Tom in a way I'd never been able to talk to anyone else. I felt strangely compelled to be honest with him even though I was sure that once he knew the truth he would run a mile. He didn't. He just accepted it, though he found it hard to understand. He said: 'You are beautiful.' I didn't believe him and the Voice told me not to listen to him, that he was one of 'them' – out to fatten me up. I couldn't understand why this tall, handsome, intelligent and funny man wanted to waste his time with me.

But he did.

We spent day and night together, studying together, going to the cinema and punting down Oxford's rivers, and after a few weeks we even started to go out for meals. I remember our first meal vividly. I felt a huge surge of panic as I walked towards the restaurant. The temptation to run away was huge. But I didn't. Tom was waiting for me and as I arrived he took me in his arms, quietly told me, 'It'll be OK – but we can leave any time you want to,' then took my hand and led me into the restaurant.

At first the mountain of food I was presented with appalled me. The Voice begged me not to eat it but I looked Tom in the eye, tuned into his voice as he told me one of his mum's funny stories and I started to eat. With every mouthful I felt a little stronger, and the Voice got quieter. By the time I had finished (half of) my meal, I felt like I had won an Olympic victory. For once, I felt proud rather than ashamed to have eaten. It was quite a turning point.

As the weeks passed and my body and mind got healthier with each meal, things began to get easier. I passed out less, I was able to understand my studies and I had a wonderful boyfriend who made me feel special. The Voice nagged occasionally but I was able to tune out, until the nightmares began.

I had never suffered night terrors, but suddenly sleep became a time of torture for me. Each night I would remember more and more about a night long ago when I had been taken advantage of in the cruellest way. The Man became a monster in my nightmares and I began to fear I'd walk into him around every corner. The night terrors were real memories, repressed for many years – and reliving that night left me broken and fragile. But Tom was always there. He watched me sleep, woke me as the nightmares started and held me until my screaming stopped and my breathing calmed. He held me, he loved me, he cared for me and he never went away.

The Voice, my other constant companion, told me I was disgusting and dirty. That it was my fault I had been raped as a child. It urged me to eat less, to help me lock those memories away again and make sure no man would ever want me. But I was strong. The memories that nearly broke me also helped me to start again. Suddenly, after years and years of battling with food, I knew WHY my battles had begun. There was a reason. It didn't make for comfortable conversation and I couldn't bring myself to talk to anyone but Tom about it, but there was a real reason for my difficulties, and it was something I could slowly start to work through.

The Voice told me I was ugly and stupid and should starve myself to death, but Tom told me I was beautiful and lovable and that I should embrace life and enjoy it with him.

In the end, deciding whom to listen to wasn't a difficult choice at all.

# 17

# Bulimia and EDNOS

## Gill Ryan

*Eating Disorders Not Otherwise Specified, or EDNOS, is a term used to describe eating disorders that do not fall into the strict categories of anorexia nervosa or bulimia nervosa. Don't be misled if you learn your illness is 'not anorexia' or 'not really bulimia'. Half of all eating disorder cases fall into the EDNOS category and outcomes in EDNOS are no less serious. In addition, the same patient may transition in and out of the EDNOS category over time. EDNOS is a serious mental illness that occurs in adults, adolescents and children. Common presentations include extremely disturbed eating habits, a distorted body image and an intense fear of gaining weight.*

*What people suffering from an eating disorder need most is hope and Gill Ryan excels in providing this. She is always happy to share her story to prove that it is possible to recover, no matter how long you have had an eating disorder. These days Gill is 'retired' and if you think that means doing nothing then think again, for she is busy as ever. Gill has great fun with her grandchildren. She counts herself lucky to have a loving and accepting husband, enjoys long walks with her two dogs and swims daily. Gill is the first woman CEO of her local bowls club and is secretly proud to have broken that glass ceiling. As for food, it has taken its natural place in her life and no longer dominates her every moment. This is Gill's story:*

As an 18-year-old student in the 1960s I came up with every sort of excuse for not eating:

'I have just had breakfast/lunch.'

'I am meeting my friend for lunch.'

'I have a dodgy stomach.'

'I'm not hungry at present.'

'I'll have something later (never!).'

All this when I was starving hungry and longing to get home and binge.

I wasn't very good at vomiting – the Voice told me I wasn't even any good at that. So I mainly chewed up food and spat it out. I caused drains to be blocked all over England. The best thing for vomiting was porridge with cream and syrup.

I bought food especially for that purpose – of course it was mainly sweet foods like cream cakes and bars of chocolate. The texture had to be right as well or else all that chewing of food would make my mouth sore. I especially liked food with raisins in it. I would pick out all the raisins and chew them first then spit them out.

I stole food from friends at college and was constantly preoccupied with food and concerned about getting thinner. I couldn't understand my behaviour because I knew I was kind, cared about my friends and was an 'A' student. I was always popular with boys so why, when I got down to my low goal weight, did I have no boyfriends at all? My reasoning was that the thinner I became the more attractive and 'good' I would become.

Of course I rotted my teeth away and had dentures at 40. All this bingeing and purging cost a great deal of money. I felt I had to do it at least once a day so holidays with the family were very stressful. I tried so hard to stop doing it as I thought it was like smoking – something I could stop if I really wanted. WRONG. It was only after the years of therapy that the need to binge and purge gradually faded and disappeared.

I became a master at hiding my bingeing. After my marriage, the kitchen became my domain at home and the children knew they were unwelcome in there.

When I was a teenager, and eating almost compulsively, I thought the food was 'calling' me to eat it. My mother noticed that food was disappearing from the kitchen but had no idea what I was doing with it.

I seemed to be totally unable to resist cheese and when I was losing weight lived almost entirely on cheese. But I couldn't let myself eat cheese like anyone else. My Voice insisted I could only eat the cheese rind – local shops at that time sold bags of assorted cheese off cuts including lots of rind! I would cut my weighed out cheese into tiny pieces and eat them very slowly.

One Christmas my mother bought a huge amount of cheese and put it in the fridge hoping, I know, that I would eat it. When I saw how much was there, I panicked. The thought of all this cheese calling me when I was stuck indoors over the chilly holiday period was a nightmare. So I took the cheese, cut it up into pieces and put it into two Marks and Spencer carrier bags. I took the train to London Bridge Station, went into the Ladies Restroom and fed the pieces of cheese down each toilet bowl. Of course the pieces were too big to flush away. I caught the train home and had to face my mother's questions. I often wonder what the cleaners thought that night when they went to clean those toilets. This behaviour, driven by the Voice, made me feel as if I was really 'mad' but I can see the funny side now.

## Food

When I first dieted I cut out all sweet stuff and carbohydrates, as was the fashion in those days. My diet was reasonable and healthy.

Once at college and in total charge of what I ate, I ate less and less, skipping meals and eating mainly fruit and vegetables.

After my gran died it all got worse. I didn't seem to know what I was doing. All I did know was that I could do my academic work and worked very hard at my studies. If I made a mistake of any sort on a page I had to rewrite it all over again. It had to be perfect.

I preferred to eat alone. If I had people around I didn't need food. Alone, I was desperate for it.

It was in this way that my boyfriends disappeared – food was such a preoccupation that I would avoid dates in case I was faced with having to eat.

Things went from bad to worse. I was admitted to the Maudsley Hospital in London and celebrated my twenty-first birthday there in 1963. I was in hospital for eight months – the physician diagnosed anorexia but gave no explanation. At that time, the illness was unheard of outside the medical profession.

Because I didn't know what anorexia meant it was much longer before the 'penny dropped'. For years I just thought I was 'mad' or peculiar. I didn't realize I actually had an illness until I trained as a marriage guidance counsellor in the mid-1980s.

When released from the Maudsley, I was still quite sick. I lived on a few tomatoes a day for a while. However I did get some work and met some kind, loving colleagues and this somehow helped me to keep fairly well by increasing my food range a little. I began to socialize and met the man who would be my first husband. I could not work out how this man could possibly find me attractive. He accepted my weird eating habits although he didn't know about the bingeing – ever.

Well, we married, I reached a reasonable weight but remained very bulimic in secret for the next 23 years. My husband never knew about the bulimia. I seemed to be battling weight gain constantly but in a different way to when I was more anorexic. Eating disorders do seem to blend into each other and sometimes you can be more anorexic and other times more bulimic. Bulimia was expensive and I denied myself new clothes and personal thing to offset the guilt of all that wasted food. My marriage crumbled, not because of the bulimia but in spite of it! It was yet another abusive relationship; in my first 45 years I had learned nothing about looking after myself. I had managed to bring up my three children but I am sure I was emotionally unavailable to them much of the time.

Now the children know my story I have been able to say 'sorry' to them and have been rewarded with much love and understanding.

I produced good meals for my family but I would eat maybe a plate of cabbage or a few other vegetables. This was a terrible example to my children and enabled the Voice to tell me what a lousy mother I was. When I talk to my children about it now, it's interesting to hear them say that they just accepted that was how things were. In secret, of course, I would binge and purge. I didn't know it then, but you keep some of those calories however hard you try. So I wasn't thin any more. I managed to have three healthy children although I did have another child, at term, who died after 12 hours. The baby, a boy, was born on my father's birthday and died on his birthday. There was a great deal of internal dialogue about this being my fault.

## Relationships

I always felt that my mother didn't like me: indeed she told me once she hated me, perhaps out of exasperation. She didn't seem to notice I was sick. It was my father who took me to see our GP when I was losing weight. My mother never showed any emotions and I suspect was depressed for most of her life.

My father and I were extremely close until I started to grow up and wasn't cute any more. I adored him and he broke my heart. When I was a teenager he hit me often, called me his 'hard bitch' daughter and, one night when I was in our kitchen drinking coffee with a boyfriend, he called me 'whore'.

My poor sense of self meant that I had absolutely no ability to defend myself in front of my parents. Eventually I coped within by telling myself: 'Whatever you do to me you're never going to hurt me again.' Dad had a great sense of humour in his early years but his shows of angry and violent emotions were scary. At about 18 I decided to 'switch off' to both parents and that's when I started to diet.

My brother and I had no relationship at all. He was five years older than me. He was 'perfect' and I was the opposite. I now know that being the perfect one has its own problems! My brother never showed any emotion. When my beloved gran died he sent me a typewritten letter informing me of her death and telling me it wasn't necessary to come down from college for the funeral.

My gran had got me through. I adored her. She was loving and kind and had a terrific sense of the ridiculous. I spent a long time with her and saw her every day. I wished I could live with her. I knew she loved me. When she died, my eating disorder took over completely.

Friends teased that I was 'fat' and they ordered catalogues to be sent to me from companies selling corsets and oversize clothes. That was their joke. It wasn't very funny when the catalogues were still coming and I was a size six. As the illness took hold I became more and more isolated. I regretted this but the Voice was too strong.

## Sense of self

As emotions were a 'no go' zone in my family, a sense of self was hard to establish. I was a lively, bright child but my parents seemed to feel a need to 'keep me down'. My father couldn't cope with me growing up and he first beat me after he caught me spitting out of my bedroom window (such a lovely clicking noise as the spit landed!). I don't know if my mother knew what he'd done and I never discussed it with anyone. I did however become school phobic and stopped eating properly – I was only eight.

At 11 my body really let me down as I almost literally exploded into puberty over a very short period. I rapidly developed large breasts and became large everywhere else too. My father and his friends were merciless in their mockery, calling me Jane (Mansfield) and Sabrina after two starlets famous for their large breasts at that time. I felt humiliated and quite mortified and hated my body, which was causing me such misery. As a result of this I might add I was unable to even contemplate breastfeeding any of my children, which gave the Voice yet another opportunity to remind me of my inadequacy.

So as a teenager I felt like an outsider in my body, which was 'fat', and I was not allowed to wear attractive clothes or grow my hair. My father cut it himself in a sort of pudding basin style. My friends were morphing into attractive people getting boyfriends and doing interesting things. I felt left out and often depressed. I ate a great deal and felt I was like a vacuum cleaner sucking up all the food around me. My diaries are full of lists of what I have eaten and what I shouldn't have eaten and why couldn't I control this enormous hunger.

My father invaded my privacy and my sense of self by entering my bedroom when I was undressing and coming into the bathroom when I was in the bath. Locks were not allowed. I learnt to cope by splitting myself into my head and my body and switching off when he was around. Over the years I met with quite a bit of sexual abuse and the same technique got me through.

Gradually I realized that to survive you have to cover up your extreme vulnerability and grow thick skin. It didn't pay to let anyone see how you hurt inside.

Only I didn't realize at the time that this was a false self.

Everyone thought I was confident, intelligent and able: I went on a diet, lost weight and felt even better. I felt less depressed, more acceptable, had a boyfriend. I honestly thought I was the person I had tried to become.

Then I had to lose more weight or the depression came back, together with the sense of being worthless, of being no good and, as the Voice in my head said: 'a total waste of space'.

I gradually shrank into a tiny nothing person with a relentless dialogue in my head saying I didn't deserve to eat, to feel good or to enjoy life.

The Maudsley Hospital helped me to see that others have this sort of dialogue. I was determined to get better but all that happened was that anorexia transitioned into bulimia and EDNOS. These other two illnesses were not as obvious and people stopped worrying about my health.

Believe me, it was just as bad. The man I married was very like my parents. He hated 'emotions', liked to keep me down and humiliated and belittled me in front of my children. I had no coping strategies and always felt powerless. 'What a fraud I am,' the Voice told me. Everyone apart from my family thought I was a strong survivor, able to stand up for anyone (sadly, not myself).

Eventually, at the age of 46, I had an affair with a man who taught me to love my body. I owe him a great debt of gratitude and we remain friends. This was a start and then years of therapy taught me to join my head with my body again and get to know that sad child within, and grieve for her. I had such a backlog of tears to shed it seemed to go on forever.

I am quite secure in who I am today. I even love my 'bad' bits.

## Treatment

Most of my therapy, which began in my forties, involved getting rid of the false extremely brave me and getting in touch with the extremely fragile frightened person that was the real me. Although my therapist didn't actually refer to 'Ed, the Voice' in our work, much of the work addressed its constant messages.

My greatest asset, I always felt, was my ability to make people laugh – my ace coping device. I tried this with the therapist, of course. But after six months she stopped laughing completely. Then the work really started.

We talked about my childhood, and onwards, for more than two years, resurrecting all the feelings I had deflected with my eating disorder and concentration on food. I resolutely refused to cry.

The therapist said I was like a big tank of water filling slowly all the time but only dripping over the side a little bit. Then one day she said in an exasperated way: 'Gill, you don't have to be brave all the time.'

That did it and the tank gushed over! I cried for months. At last I had found the real person inside me and, you know, she wasn't as bad as the Voice made out. Gradually I learnt, when the Voice said, 'You don't deserve this or that,' to reply: 'Rubbish.' But for a long time the Voice still managed to get through, saying: 'You're not that great; you're too full of yourself.' That was the hardest thing – allowing myself to actually like myself.

So there it is – more than 30 years of 'eating distress'. Have I really recovered? Well, I still get bad patches but no longer panic as I have strategies on board now to help me cope. I remain super-sensitive but understand this is a common personality trait among people who develop anorexia. The bad patches are always associated with unresolved feelings, and I have learnt to seek them out and talk about them, and somehow food doesn't seem so important.

The feelings that cause most problems are usually associated with feeling hurt and powerless. Fortunately I can talk to my current husband about how I feel – he doesn't say much but he knows how much just saying the words helps. He accepts me exactly as I am and expects nothing more from me. That's a big help.

There are some things I still feel too anxious to do – like go to dinner parties, although I can eat out in restaurants. I have just been away for two weeks' holiday in New Zealand. For the first time in my life I managed to eat out every night and actually enjoy it! Work still in progress eh?

## Reflection

I read a story years ago that went like this:

> 'A woman had severe agoraphobia and was so depressed she decided to commit suicide. She decided to get in her car and just drive. This was the worst thing she could imagine doing as she'd rarely left the house for years. She knew that this would be the end of her. In desperation she got in the car and just drove on and on and on and on…she didn't die but just drove. Then she knew that agoraphobia wouldn't kill her.'

Eating disorders are a bit like this: to recover, you just have to keep pushing on and on. When you face your greatest fear head on nothing terrible ever really happens and eventually you are sure that eating a cream bun won't actually make you fat. Recovery is a bit like mourning. You have to go through it; you can't go round it and come out successfully.

Freedom from that Voice feels like Julie Andrews looks at the beginning of the movie, *The Sound of Music*. You have so much more space in your head to do and learn and enjoy. I regret all the time I have wasted listening to that Voice.

## Persevere – you never know when a crack in Ed may appear

As mentioned, after the breakdown of my first marriage, I trained as a marriage guidance counsellor – ironic but true. People had always found it easy to talk to me about personal matters, so I thought I might as well use this 'talent'. At this point I realized I had to sort myself out before I could help others. This was when I was lucky to find a therapist who specialized in eating disorders and she helped me over four years to untangle the sorry web of my life. It was a revelation and I wished I had been given the chance of such help earlier.

I have since spent a long time in the UK counselling young women with eating problems. I soon realized that each person has a different story and their own path to travel to find good health again. Small wonder a definitive 'cure' has not been found. I am certain that the finest resources we have are people like me who have recovered and who can offer hope and understanding to sufferers.

I feel passionately for eating disorder sufferers carrying on bravely, alone in their misery. I have met many middle-aged women, all of them remarkable. Of course the young people should have all the care and attention they need. However, the many mothers struggling with bulimia and EDNOS are the silent majority.

# 18

# Binge Eating Disorder

## Chevese Turner

I am thrilled to share my story here. A life of recovery, for me, is participating in continual self-care, recognizing where boundaries need to be set in various areas of life, and a consistent willingness to change and evolve in the relationship I have with myself and others. I believe this approach is the key to sustained recovery.

My life continues to thrive in many ways and within the context of recovery. I have a wonderful, supportive husband and two beautiful, big-hearted sons. Family life is my priority and it is supported by a network of friends, family and others who are part of my 'recovery circle'. I founded the Binge Eating Disorder Association in 2008 and this has met my need to help others and I am expanding my involvement in providing treatment and access to care for those struggling with eating disorders. The promise of recovery was not sold short for me, but was neither an easy nor a short journey. I am grateful for every bump in the road and even the detours that at times took me out of the way. Recovery is a gift to myself that is self-actualizing and I am forever thankful.

It is effortless for me to acknowledge that I have binge eating disorder (BED) at this point in my life. After years of silent shame, I now understand the purpose the disorder served. This knowledge gave me the ability to be a whole person and map my future without having to consider a never-ending preoccupation with food.

It wasn't always this way. Some time between the ages of five and seven, I discovered the power of food. I discovered I wanted more of it than I was permitted to have, that it was a restricted temptation, and that I thought about it a lot. It calmed and shamed me at the same time. It signified love and hate. It brought me up and then down. It was my best friend and my worst enemy.

As a child, aged four to twelve, I liked to play with friends but would often lead my playmates to the kitchen hoping they would ask a parent for food. I did not like to ask for food. I was ashamed, even at an early age, of my seemingly insatiable appetite, because I was sure I was the only person struggling this way. I was strangely 'abnormal' in my mind and this created a gap between the rest of the world and me early on.

Usually a binge began with an opportunity to access food during a time that I was bored or feeling like I needed something to fill the space during an unsettling moment. My first memory is at age five, stealing ice cream cones (without the ice cream) from a kitchen cabinet and stashing them in my bedroom. Later in the day I sat in my room with the door closed and ate several of the cones until I was so sick I felt as if I would vomit.

During this initial period I thought about food often throughout my day and was very preoccupied by when and what I would eat. Many times binges began in my head long before the opportunity to eat. Typically binges were whatever was accessible when an adult was not looking. More often than not, it was handfuls of candy, crackers, ice cream cones (without ice cream), pretzels or chips. The amount usually comprised a handful or two of food – whatever I could grab and eat quickly. When there was an opportunity to stash food, it would be as much as I could consume before feeling sick. At this young age it was ten to twenty crackers, several candy bars or five or six ice cream cones. The binge was brief – usually it was over within ten minutes. It could be longer if I had a sizeable stash and was left alone. I stopped eating when I ran out of food, was caught eating when I was not permitted to, or when I began to feel sick.

Before eating I usually felt agitated and anxious: I could not wait to eat. During eating I was calm and even though my stomach would begin to feel uncomfortable, my mind felt calm and almost disconnected: it was not processing anything but the smell and taste of the food, which was a relief. After eating, I would be even more agitated and could focus only on how full my stomach felt and how tired and sluggish my body felt. Emotionally I felt depleted – sad and angry.

My mother insisted that I 'eat healthy' and taught me to distinguish between 'good' and 'bad' food early in my childhood. She had her own problems with food. For her, it was love, but also a source of control. She learned during her own difficult childhood and teenage years that she had power over food and herself if she denied hunger. She was probably anorexic, although she was never officially diagnosed or treated. She went on to abuse alcohol in her twenties and thirties, and unknowingly passed all her shameful feelings about her body to me.

From the age of eight to fourteen, I struggled with the stigma of being overweight. I was teased and bullied despite being well liked by my peers and teachers. My parents explained that they were concerned for me and tried many interventions. My mother and I dieted together with little success and I learned to rely on the scale to determine how I felt about myself. An entire day, week or month could be ruined by a weight gain and I correlated these gains to my inability to be 'good'. It was difficult to enjoy life while concentrating on how not to think about food.

My deep-seated guilt about the secret eating binges produced a lot of anxiety and depression. I knew that people wondered how I could gain weight while eating normal portions at meals and that my overweight body was a source of anxiety and helplessness for my parents. I was ashamed that I could not keep myself away from food and yet it was the only thing that allowed me to escape and simultaneously calm me during tumultuous family times and the normal stresses of everyday life.

As my weight continued to increase through childhood and into my adolescence, I withdrew from friends and activities. My mother's alcoholism and my parents' eventual divorce took a toll on me. I spent my teenage years engaging in risky behaviour and bingeing on food, alcohol and, to some extent, drugs. Food was always the preferred substance. I planned each binge I could, but was always open to the spontaneous consumption of whatever was available.

During my late teens and early twenties, I realized that my friends and high school classmates were going on to college and building their lives. I attempted twice to attend college and found that I could not handle the pressure and resulting anxiety and depression that came with the demands of a higher education. This failure, in my perfectionist mind, was unforgivable.

I struggled for several more years, from age 22 to 24, but my mental health deteriorated and my waistline expanded. I was in the depth of despair and depression with no money, no future and even less sense of self. I knew that I needed help and that it meant a commitment to searching for answers. I was not hopeful, but willing to try anything.

I found a weight management programme and, with the help of a therapist, began to work on the underlying issues related to my eating binges. At the time, binge eating disorder was not mentioned as a diagnosis, and I was confused about whether I had an eating disorder or a lack of willpower. At the end of the day, it did not matter: I was losing weight and feeling better than ever before. I felt my problems were melting along with the weight.

During my late twenties, cognitive-behavioural therapy provided me with a new outlook on life and tools that I could take with me. I began a university programme in political science and began engaging in life. I was managing considerably better, but only temporarily. During the four years at university, more than half of the pounds I had lost found me again. It was a sign that I had not fully conquered my eating problems. I knew that I needed to seek treatment again.

At age 29, a new therapist diagnosed me with 'binge eating disorder'. I cannot convey the liberation I felt. All my food preoccupation and overeating actually had a name and I could stop making moral judgements about myself. I was finally able to look at the problem and find ways to address it without guilt and shame. Responsibility for the disorder now belonged to me and I felt relief.

I assumed this diagnosis meant that there were many more people who struggled like me. I began to search for other binge eaters through both national and local eating disorder groups. Occasionally I found one or two, but it soon became apparent that either I was one of a very few or that this disorder was severely under-diagnosed and under-discussed. Certain that it was the latter, I began to think about what it would be like to have a supportive community of people with binge eating disorder. At the time, I had no idea how this unmet need in the eating disorder community would directly affect the direction of my life.

Over the next ten years I married a wonderful and supportive man, had two children, and continued to work on my recovery. I learned that dieting was contributing to my inability to let go of the disorder, but continued to struggle with what to do about my excess weight and burgeoning health problems.

In early 2007, at age 40, and after a particularly difficult year, I opted for lap-band surgery. The day after I returned home from the hospital, I began to have serious withdrawal from food. I obsessed about it, cried, screamed, and became very depressed. I couldn't believe that after all these years of therapy and self-discovery food could still control me like this. It was clear that this band around my stomach was not going to solve my problems. I would need to continue my work with a treatment team to address all of the issues that come with BED, including depression, anxiety, inner-child issues, food preoccupation, physical health ailments, sleep disturbances and body image to name a few.

I assembled my team to include a psychologist, nutritionist and several complementary practitioners who help me manage anxiety through massage, acupuncture and exercise. My therapist used a combination of cognitive-behavioural, dialectical-behavioural, and interpersonal-behavioural therapies. We addressed my relationships, the emotional needs I have that were not being met, and how to listen to my body. We also worked to improve my body image, which has taken a beating over the years. I began to accept what I see in the mirror by focusing on me as a person and not me as defined by the size I am or the need to live up to another person's ideal about body shape or size.

At the same time, my primary care physician introduced me to intuitive eating and this became a powerful tool as I addressed my relationship with food. It allowed me to identify my body's nutritional needs independent of what my mind was craving. It also allowed me to identify when I was hungry or when I was trying to fill some unmet emotional need. It required me to step away from the TV or the computer while eating and to recognize when my stomach was beginning to feel like it had enough. It eased the preoccupation and removed the space for perfectionism, dichotomous thinking, shame and dieting.

Learning to eat intuitively was not easy. It is a skill and there were times I doubted it could work for me. Early on, I continued to hang on to weight loss as the ultimate goal in recovery. What I did not understand was that weight loss as a goal was actually getting in the way of helping my body find its healthy weight. It was feeding back in to the preoccupation with food and how much or little of it I should eat. It set me up for binges as it triggered my feelings of shame around how I looked.

Now in my mid-forties, I no longer focus on weight, but rather on the positive things I can do for my body on a daily basis. My nutritionist helps guide me to the foods that I am leaving out of my diet. She encourages me to add and never asks me to take anything away. She helps me practise understanding what I need and suggests ideas for trying foods I do not like or do not include in my diet. With this work I have begun to enjoy a better balanced diet and the cravings for high sugar and fat content food have decreased.

This said there are times when, even now, I binge. After more than 35 years of practising bingeing as a coping mechanism I have perfected its utility. The difference now is that I recognize the binges. They look very different than they did in my earlier years, but they feel the same. The quantity is much less and I am able to catch myself mid-binge. Certain foods, situations and people can contribute to the internal swell toward a binge. I am patient with myself, as I know I cannot possibly be perfect and that one binge does not mean that I have failed miserably. I adjust post-binge and continue down the road of life.

My therapist continues to help me address the binge episodes by confronting the triggers and getting to the heart of what the food holds for me emotionally. Usually, it is the need for self-care, a difficult relationship, or a boundary I have not set. Certain times of the day continue to be difficult. Evenings before bed are troublesome for me. I now understand that this probably means I need some self-care and more than likely a hug from my husband. I have learned to ask for the hug and acknowledge the needs, which goes a long way toward diffusing a binge. I also ask myself 'Am I hungry?' and then listen to the answer. It is usually no, but if I truly am hungry then I allow myself to eat to a place where I am comfortable.

I continue to explore what works for me and to learn to soothe my inner self with something other than food. I allow my imperfections in all their beauty and embrace my body at every size along the way.

I no longer weigh myself but continue to lose weight as is evidenced by my clothing size.

I continue to work with my treatment team regularly, and engage in activities I enjoy, such as biking, swimming and gardening.

I now believe, based on my own experience, that at its core, BED is not about the weight. Weight is a by-product of all the reasons a binge eater began to use food to comfort and soothe. It is the replacement for what is missing on the inside. It is a response and perhaps a malfunction in wiring, but it is not the single identifying factor for those of us who struggle with the disorder.

Millions of people with binge eating disorder suffer in silence. It is very important that the primary care provider community listen closely to the messages that are subtly sent by each person who is eating disordered. A person who struggles with depression and/or anxiety should be screened for an eating disorder along with all other possible mental health conditions; people who appear withdrawn or are consistently gaining or losing weight should be examined and followed closely; and every person who presents as overweight or obese should have a full physical and mental health evaluation as this person could quite possibly be one of the 40 per cent of overweight or obese people who have binge eating disorder.

My life has changed completely from those days of shame and hopelessness. I am now a whole person who refuses to hide my struggles or me. The Binge Eating Disorder Association (BEDA – website www.bedaonline.com) has enabled me to build the community I dreamt of all those years ago. It is my hope that the millions who suffer will have a place where they can discover they are not alone and can indeed learn to build their own path to recovery with the help of the treatment provider community and the awareness, education and advocacy BEDA provides.

# 19

## Anorexia

### Kelly Richards

*Simple things give Kelly pleasure: her sunny-natured, blonde two-year-old leaping out of the broom cupboard with a big 'Boo Mummy!'; her four-year-old carefully balancing his recycled creations as he walks through the kindergarten gates; and her six-year-old putting his runners on the wrong feet in his haste to play football with his mates. To others travelling the recovery path, Kelly says: 'Hang on – hang on – keep going – you'll get there too!'*

My eldest son, at his kindergarten Christmas concert, glanced at me from under his floppy reindeer ears, looking like he'd way prefer to be outside kicking a football than standing before a bunch of mothers and grandparents with camcorders. His look reminded me of those hard years of recovery from anorexia. Every day that I had cried uncontrollably, pulled at my hair, felt hopeless and prayed desperately to anyone who would listen to help free me from the torment, had led to this moment of being a proud mother in the kindergarten.

My son's fifth birthday earlier that year had coincided with the tenth anniversary of when I first sat in a psychologist's chair, attempting to convince her that I wasn't supposed to be there. I had all but screamed: 'I'm not skinny enough to have anorexia.' The diagnosis proved otherwise. I was aged 27.

I had battled anorexia in silence since my early teens. Not that I'm about to bore you with the details that come with several emotionally agonizing years of counselling. I've wasted enough time psychoanalysing my stereotypical anorexic past (perfectionist, eldest, high-achiever, low self-esteem). Instead I will focus on the part when you have recovered sufficiently from anorexia to walk in the community alone, meet a loving partner, get married and have kids. What is life like? Does recovery hold strong with the stress that comes with pregnancy, weight gain, miscarriage and three children under five?

I'm sure there are many mothers out there, like me, who have recovered sufficiently from their illness, and are going quietly about the business of school and kindergarten pick-ups, playgroups, chatting to neighbours, balancing work, study, family, relationships and generally keeping oneself fed.

Motherhood on the whole has had a positive effect on my eating disorder. I consider myself 'normal' (after a lifetime of feeling 'different'), given I now eat a variety of food and regular meals and no longer feel compelled to exercise every single day. More importantly, I'm realistic about what I can achieve and no longer suffer from non-stop negative self-talk. Mostly I am grateful that I have been able to produce three healthy children with a body that I starved, tortured and hated. In fact, my children have delivered the toughest self-image, self-renewal boot camp that three years of sitting opposite a psychologist armed with a notepad and pen could never have provided.

Not that it has all been smooth sailing. As with most recovery stories, I've had my share of setbacks. Anorexia is renowned for sneaking up from behind and grabbing you in a silent headlock no matter how smart you consider yourself to be. It starts with a missed lunch, then a smaller dinner than usual, and the next thing you know you have hardly eaten all week. Times of stress, crisis or change are when I am at my most vulnerable.

With my first baby, I became distressed after four weeks when I hadn't regained my size and hit the pavement desperate to lose the baby-weight I had gained. Even after several years of being 'well', the anorexia thoughts and behaviours resurged and became my way of coping with fear and change. Of course, it didn't work. I wanted to gain back 'control' over my body and had to somehow deal with the incredibly inadequate feelings and fears that accompanied the launch into motherhood. After giving birth to a second baby, I found myself sitting before a doctor in a small coastal town, with a 15-month-old and a crying newborn, listening to a description of my anaemia and being forced to explain (while fetching dummies from the floor and pulling a toddler away from a medical bin) that despite my 'coping' presentation, what I really needed was a referral to my psychologist as once again, I was struggling to eat.

I've found that recovery from anorexia has some similarities with motherhood. It can be tough at times; a constant evolving process of growth; redefining what is important, what makes for happiness and maintaining a balance between my needs and that of my busy family.

For you see, some of my closest 'new' friends know nothing of my past. Mostly they are other mothers and neighbours that I have met during the course of my children attending kindergarten and school. While I tell myself that there hasn't been much of an opportunity to confide, the truth is that I cherish being perceived as 'normal'. A decade after recovery from anorexia, I still fear being instantly redefined in the eyes of others who know about it. That I will be watched more closely at a party (I still struggle to eat in the smallest of crowds), greater meaning will be extracted from what I say, or comments will be made if my jeans are hanging loosely or I refuse a piece of cake. My biggest fear is that all that I have achieved could be taken away; that the tormenting voice of anorexia will convince me again that I don't deserve such happiness.

My children counterbalance this fear. They teach me to be more human, rather than a super impersonator of someone who is perfect and always keeping the balls in the air. Kids are messy, get sick, don't use their manners (especially when you most want them to) and state their opinions out loud.

My four-year-old son summed my feelings up perfectly when he came into my bed in the middle of the night. He cuddled up and muffled in my ear that he had had a bad dream but now that he was snuggled close to me, all his thoughts were 'happy thoughts'. 'Me too, me too,' I said as I felt the warmth of his breath and the softening of his body as he drifted back to sleep. Such moments make for the happy ending I prayed for and I cling to them. 'Here and now' moments keep me well.

# 20

## Anorexia and Bulimia

### June Alexander

*Genetic, biological and personality traits contribute to the vulnerability of developing an eating disorder. Add an environmental trigger, such as intense anxiety or trauma, and the illness can take off. June reflects on her experience:*

My childhood was in many ways idyllic, growing up on a dairy farm in Australia in the 1950s. Outside influences were minimal – the farmhouse didn't have electricity until I was 11 years old; there were no household labour-saving appliances like washing machines and certainly no television. I had one older sister. She had long hair and I had short hair. I grew up as a tomboy, which I loved. Given that I had been a difficult birth and my mother was unable to have more children, I was the closest to a boy that my parents were going to get to help on the farm. This suited me fine as I was happiest outdoors with my dad. My mother called me 'Tim' when I was good and 'Toby' when I was not so good. I grew up feeling that I was never quite what she wanted.

One day, just after my eleventh birthday, I got my first period. I hadn't noticed anything wrong when I got out of bed that morning and took off to the dairy to help my dad. It was the summer holidays and I was in a rush to do my farm jobs so I could play with my boy cousins when they got up. I'd never been told about periods, so it was a real shock when I went back to the house after feeding the calves and my mother called me into her bedroom. She had found some blood when she went to make my bed and now she was talking about periods. She handed me a folded baby's nappy pinned to a thin elasticized belt. I had to put this on, pull my shorts over the top and return to the dairy to wash the yards out for my father. I feared Dad would see the big bulge through my shorts. I felt like my whole world had caved in. 'This is going to happen every month for the rest of my life,' I thought. I had planned a cricket match and swimming that day with my city cousins who were staying for the holidays but my mother said: 'You can't go swimming while you are bleeding.' I was devastated.

A few weeks later the new school year began. I was in year six and my breasts had begun to develop more. One Monday morning all the students were standing in a line in front of the flagpole to sing the national anthem. We had to put our hand over our heart while we sang *God Save the Queen*. I could feel my breast bumps and looked down the line and everyone else's chests were flat. I was the only girl in the school with breasts. I hated them. I loved to play cricket and football with the boys but now I had to hold my breasts when I ran, or they hurt. I hated them and I hated that the teacher could see.

One day, the teacher, who was also my cousin, announced that the doctor was coming to the school. Being in the country, the doctor visited about once every four years. I began to feel very anxious. I would have to undress so the doctor could examine me and I didn't want to do this with my cousin anywhere near. I told my mother and sister that I didn't want to see the doctor. 'Don't be silly,' they said. 'All the other girls are doing it, you'll be fine.' But I didn't feel fine and had no one else to talk to. Soon after that, one day during lunch break at school I was sitting on the grass in the playground. Something in my brain went 'ping' and from that day on I stopped eating.

I started running everywhere. My mother felt embarrassed because people saw me running up and down the country roads, even in the rain. I threw my lunch away to the farm animals or gave it to other children at school. At dinner I would sneak food off my plate, putting it in my pockets under the tablecloth or on to someone else's plate when they weren't looking. I became very thin very quickly. The school doctor came and went but I could not eat. Anorexia had developed but there was no diagnosis and no treatment.

My mother got angry at my stubbornness. She took great pride in cooking wholesome meals and could not understand why I refused to eat them. I wanted to please her but the fear of eating was too great. Even though I rather miraculously began eating about 18 months after anorexia developed, and my family assumed I was well, things weren't right. One effect of developing anorexia had been the gradual cessation of menstruation and this had not restarted. After three years without a period my mother took me to the local doctor. He prescribed the Pill, which made me gain about seven kilograms in three months. My hormones went crazy. When the medication ceased, my periods stopped again, so the doctor put me on the Pill for another six months. I felt bloated and uncomfortable with this new body. This time my period returned to stay but my health remained compromised. I went through high school achieving high grades, coping with anxiety by restricting food intake, exercising excessively, bingeing, feeling confused, depressed and isolated; I felt on the periphery, rather than within, my group of friends.

Although I did not feel it, I was popular at school – in the school hockey team, a school prefect, a cross-country running champion and top academic student. Friends encouraged me to be more outgoing and, at age 16, I met George, who became my boyfriend. All the while, I continued to secretly binge, and punish myself through restriction and exercise.

I had always loved writing so when I finished high school, which included a year as an exchange student in the United States, I landed a job as a cadet journalist at the local newspaper. At age 20, I married George. I fainted the morning of our wedding, as I had not eaten. Eight weeks into married life, after bingeing on ten scones for breakfast, my car collided with a loaded log truck on the way to work and I sustained injuries to my cervical spine. Specialists concluded it was too dangerous to operate.

I became pregnant within 12 months and had four children by the time I was 26. I tried to eat normally during each nine-month pregnancy; each pregnancy became a goal for a new start, to permanently get my eating under control. I said over and over to myself: 'By the time I have this baby I'll be eating normally and I will continue to eat normally. I'll be normal like everyone else.' But this never happened. No health professional picked up on my inner struggle. It didn't occur to me to tell my doctor, because I was sure I was just plain weak-minded, and would be told I was 'silly', and worse, not worthy of being a mother. Within a week of having a baby, despite my best efforts I'd be bingeing or starving myself again. I would be extremely upset; this in turn would upset the breast milk, causing my babies to vomit. At 26, immediately after the birth of my fourth child, I had a tubal litigation because otherwise – even though the obstetrician had been gravely concerned my fourth baby was starving in the womb – I would keep having children, in a futile attempt to gain control over an illness I did not know I had.

Now that I was unable to have more children, I entered a really dark period. Inner torment became intense. I felt that if only I could put my hand in my head I could pull out this great big black blob that seemed resident in my brain. The eating disorder's presence felt tangible. Its tentacles were squeezing the life out of me. This was a scary time, which was hard on my husband and young children. If one of the children were tapping a spoon on the table, for instance, while waiting for their dinner, I would run screaming to the other end of the house. My head felt as fragile as an egg without a shell; there was no buffer to the outside world. By now I was living in the same community where I grew up, and yet I felt isolated and disconnected, like I didn't belong, and that's when family secrets started to surface. There had been a sexual perpetrator in the family home when I was young and he had not been held accountable. Everyone but me seemed to be coping.

I tried to talk to my sister but she said: 'You've got Satan in you, you think about yourself too much.' Such comments made me feel weak and worthless, like other people could cope with life, but that I couldn't.

I appeared to have the perfect life. I had four beautiful children, a loving husband, a new home that we had built and created together, and we lived on a beautiful farm in a rich and fertile valley. I was working at the local town's newspaper in a job I loved. I had everything, but felt I was going mad. My mind would go into a space all of its own. One night, I was screaming and the children were hiding under their beds. Unable to take the inner pain any more, I was hitting my head against the wall, trying to numb the pain. My husband and I both knew I needed help. It was time to stop kidding myself that this was something I could manage, and should be able to manage, alone.

I had feared that if I told a doctor what was going on inside my head, insanity would be confirmed, and my children would be taken from me. But now the children inspired me to move beyond this fear and hang on to a desire to live; for their sake I had to be brave and seek help. The hometown doctor listened as I tried to explain what my life had come to, and he said reassuringly: 'This is obviously something that happened during a difficult birth. Look, your battery's flat. You're a cougar not a cat. Don't worry, we've got medication to get you back on track.' He sent me home with a prescription. I thought, 'Oh great, I will be normal now.' But the pills didn't help. The doctor didn't realize that the eating disorder was the core problem and my mental health went from bad to worse.

Six years of misdiagnosis followed. A clinical psychologist decided I was severely hypoglycaemic and recommended a special diet. That didn't help either. The eating disorder played games and I used the times between sessions to weigh less by the next appointment. Different medications were prescribed, the side-effects including nausea, severe headaches and confusion.

During this time, social isolation increased. I felt incapable compared with other mothers of young children in the farming district. They seemed carefree, so why couldn't I be like that too? They could eat a cream cake and laugh when we gathered at the mothers' group. I didn't know an eating disorder was controlling my mind and that what I was experiencing were its symptoms.

My thoughts were taken up with worrying about what I would eat for the next meal and planning new strategies to break the binge–starve cycle. I relied on calorie counting to cope with working full time at the newspaper office and caring for four children under the age of six.

For 20 years, my weight had been see-sawing. I felt fat, no matter what I weighed. I had a goal weight which was like a magnet, the centre of my being. 'If I get to this amount, everything in my life will be OK,' I'd think every day. 'My world will be all right, I won't feel tormented; I'll manage everything.' But I would reach this goal weight and everything would not be all right. It obviously was not the answer to overcoming the torment. It got to the stage where I would binge and literally knock myself out, sleeping for hours and feeling terrible for the next few days until I had the will to start afresh. Striving to reach that goal weight yet again, striving to silence the tormenting voice in my head.

At age 32, I saw a new psychiatrist. Immediately I thought, 'This man can help me.' He prescribed a medication that saved my life in a way, because it numbed my brain while I worked on recovery, but it also seemed to alter my thoughts and subsequent behaviours. Suddenly the eating disorder behaviours seemed to transition outwards. For the first time since meeting George I was attracted to other men. I had a brief affair with a man, convinced he was the key to beating my illness. Alas, he was aligned with it. Within ten weeks my 15-year marriage was over. George blamed the psychiatrist and the medication. The psychiatrist said I was going through a crisis.

Even though our marriage ended, George and I remained close. After our divorce, I descended further into the eating disorder and was admitted to a mental health hospital several times. I'd no sense of self. I knew I loved my children and I loved to write but didn't know anything beyond that because the eating disorder had dominated my brain for so long.

In my forties I met a dietician who talked about feelings rather than food and introduced me to a therapist, Belinda, who specialized in eating disorders and listened to my story. Belinda expressed amazement that I had survived. 'It's a miracle you are still here,' she said. That helped in a way. 'I'm here,' I thought. Belinda became pivotal to my recovery. When I was 47 years old, she said something that no one had said in all my years with an eating disorder: 'Practise separating your thoughts from the thoughts of the eating disorder.' This advice was enlightening because it helped me to see that if I could focus on my true feelings, I could regain me from the anorexia. I wasn't all bad, after all! And, most importantly, there was hope! I started to work on identifying what belonged to the eating disorder and learning to defuse those thoughts, while at the same time learning skills to cope with everyday challenges in developing the true me.

The only way I knew to cope with anxiety for more than 30 years had been to binge and purge. Learning new behaviours so that I could retrain my thoughts was a long but essential process that took place over the next eight years.

## Picking up the fragments

After my marriage with George ended, I entered several destructive relationships. One of my sons, aged 14 at the time, said insightfully: 'Mum, you're like one of those battered women you write about in the newspaper. You keep going back to be hurt more.' Deep down I knew that to recover my identity, I had to be brave enough to live alone and know me, and love me, before I could share my life with anyone else. Belinda helped me to see that my relationships since leaving George had been aligned with the eating disorder. They had been dominating, deceptive, manipulative and abusive. I had to learn skills to withstand the pull of the illness. That is what the doctors and my therapists drummed in to me. I had to learn to love myself.

Recovery edged forward on many fronts. At age 48, advances in medical technology gave a helping hand. A titanium rod was inserted into my cervical spine (replacing four vertebrae and three discs injured in the log truck accident 28 years before) and my neurosurgeon joined two psychiatrists in insisting I say a mantra: *I deserve to be treated with respect.* This eventually became an autocue in my brain; building self-belief was hard work – rebuilding this person that got lost at age 11.

Everything slowly started to come together. I made it through some awful times of rejection – like not being invited to my niece's wedding or my parents' sixtieth wedding anniversary celebrations. Many hurtful things had happened, leading to alienation from my family of origin, but my carers and treatment team gradually convinced me that I was not the problem.

The learning and applying of coping skills led to experiencing the amazing peace and contentment that comes with taking care of oneself – for the first time in decades I began to feel safe, secure and stable.

Initially, thoughts needed to be handled consciously. I had to learn to catch and defuse the Ed thoughts. Starving and bingeing was not the way to cope with feelings. 'Focus on your feelings and the food will take care of itself,' Belinda said. Learning to let entrenched behaviours go was scary as they had to be replaced with new, safe behaviours. I had to become sufficiently self-aware to say to myself: 'What's bothering me right now? What can I do to deal with this right now?' I learnt to listen to music, walk my dog, talk to God, call a friend and sort my thoughts while walking.

I had to stop counting calories and tell myself that 'I don't need to binge today because I can eat tomorrow'; that 'Even if I do binge today, I must eat tomorrow.' 'I must always eat breakfast, and lunch and dinner.' For years I had not eaten anything until six o'clock in the evening, fearing that if I started to eat, I wouldn't be able to stop. To leave the eating disorder behind, I had to eat normally and feed my brain regularly and with different foods. Many times I had despaired that I would never be able to look forward to a meal or eat three meals a day; that I wouldn't know when I was hungry or when I had eaten enough. But practice makes perfect. Since age 55, in 2006, regular meals and good nutrition have led to an amazing transformation in thought patterns. I take pleasure in feeling what my body wants, and what foods I would like to eat for my next meal. Being free of the rigidity of the illness behaviours is a luxury for which I give daily thanks.

I experienced anxiety before and after my eating disorder and medication had been a great help. However, now a far more pleasurable solution appeared – in the form of a new generation. Such is the power of love, that I have eaten three meals and three snacks every day since the birth of my first grandchild in September 2006. No more medicine required. Lucky me.

I started to become involved in the eating disorder advocacy and research field. Book research led to meeting experts in the field and learning about Maudsley Family Based Treatment for young people with anorexia. As soon as I heard about this treatment I thought: 'Oh, I wish that treatment had been around when I had been a kid; it might have saved my family.'

Looking back, I wish someone had been able to say to me before I married:

> 'Look, that torment you feel is due to eating disorder thoughts and behaviours. This is why you're feeling this way; this is why you're acting this way. You have an illness and we can help you fight it. We can give you and your family skills. Those bossy thoughts belong to the illness, and these thoughts are the real you; we're going to help you strengthen the real you.'

That would have been incredibly helpful, too.

My eldest grandchild will be seven years old next birthday. His age is the yardstick of my freedom. Regular and adequate nutrition aside, my four children and grandchildren – five of them now – are my best tonic and inspiration. My outlook on life has become 'I can' and 'I will'. This attitude is taking me on all sorts of wonderful adventures, which include, for the first time, a loving relationship without Ed. By remarkable coincidence, his name is George. Life is beautiful.

# 21

# Who Am I Without Ed?

If you are unable to envisage your life without Ed, terrified of what will be left if you let your eating disorder go, it can help to know that everyone who has recovered has felt afraid too – they got through it and so can you.

You may feel worried that there will be an awful silence and emptiness within your mind and soul, but you are a thinker, you always have been, and you will remain a big thinker. Without Ed, you will think about different and far more exciting and creative things that nurture the real you. At stressful times the temptation to go back to old coping habits may kick in, but you will develop skills to deal with these voices. The more you listen and behave according to your own true voice, the easier recovery becomes. The more you engage in life beyond your eating disorder, the more you will feel secure in believing 'Yes, I can do this!'

Children are always a great inspiration for a hopeful future. If you have no children of your own, there are many community activities you can engage in to share the joy of others. At every age, children are great deflectors of eating disorder thoughts. At the same time, you want to nurture their confidence, resilience and self-assurance. Purpose gives reason for living.

Apart from children, heaps of interests outside your Ed are waiting to be discovered and explored – hiking, cycling, craftwork, gardening, volunteer work, book clubs, creative writing, travel, study, dancing, swimming, career, decorating a home, walking the dog, dining with friends – endless rewarding pastimes, like gold at the end of your rainbow, that encourage you to engage with others and build a strong network that protects and nurtures your sense of self. No longer are you captive to the 'all or nothing' thoughts of bossy Ed. Don't wait for tomorrow to become the 'real you' – reach out, make a call, start living your life today.

## A mother's reflection (Anon)

When it got too dark in my mind and I would head towards thoughts of 'I can't do this any more' and worse, to 'ending it all', I would look at my children. Eating disorders have a large genetic influence – and despite both my parents being medically trained, their lack of realization and understanding resulted in me never getting the treatment I needed in my teens. But I can do better for my children than my parents were able to do for me. I am the best person to look out for signs of an eating disorder and I am the best person to listen when my children tell me things that are worrying them. I need to live to protect them from the monster that has dominated the last 20 years of my life. I am where the family legacy of ED ends.

## A grandmother's reflection (June Alexander)

In my twenties and thirties I made sure that my children had lots of opportunities – swimming, ballet, brownies, cubs, tennis, horse riding lessons and more. But I never once got in the pool and played with them. Or went to a dance rehearsal, or to a hockey match or gymkhana, or went camping with them. Not once. The rigidity of thought imposed by decades of eating disorders prevented me doing many things that I knew I would have enjoyed, and yearned to do, but could not allow myself to do. But today I am free to do all these things with my grandchildren. A constant joy of eating disorder recovery is the freedom to share time, real 'in the moment' time, with grandchildren, each of whom has a special knack of engaging attention.

Like the day I surprised two of my grandchildren, aged five and two. For the first time, they saw me in a bathing costume. They laughed, and so did I. They laughed a lot more when we entered the indoor swimming pool. The five-year-old had a large water pistol and proceeded to shoot me. The only thing was, he was laughing so much he could not see straight and luckily missed his target much of the time. The two-year-old, resplendent in her pink 'Tinkerbell' bathers, took to the water like the plastic yellow duck and three baby ducks that her mum had given her to play with and I was busy keeping up. Her mum was expecting baby number three in three weeks and was looking on from the poolside – she was laughing too.

For an hour we frolicked in the indoor pool like seals in the sea. Happy. Happy. Happy. Why was this simple event so important to me? Because I let it happen!

My grandson was so impressed at having my company in the pool, that when I suggested maybe it was not such a good idea to shoot Grandma in the eyes with that water pistol (because I needed to keep an eye on his little sister, proper little fish that she was), he pulled off his goggles and said: 'Here Grandma, put these on.' To be offered goggles by a young grandson is special indeed. I loved swimming as a child. Growing up by a river in rural Australia, I swam several times a day during the summer holidays – with the snakes, goannas, platypus, salamanders, bearded dragons, eels and whatever else had made its home in the river. I love water. Full stop. I love to look at it, hear the sounds (of rain, waves, rapids) and most of all, I love being in it. My grandchildren remind me of this; they are great life-coaches.

Another time, grandson Lachlan, aged five, and I took a train-ride to a children's hands-on science show, as a birthday present. On the way home he held my hand, skipped along the footpath and said: 'Oh Grandma, this has been the best day ever.'

I am glad Lachlan was focusing on his skipping (avoiding the cracks, as he does, in the concrete path), as my eyes had become rather moist; warm fuzzy feelings had enveloped me. 'This', I said to Lachlan, 'has been the "best day ever" for me, too.' We squeezed hands a little tighter, kicked up our heels, and raced for the car.

How special it is, to simply 'be'. To be a kid with my grandson, enjoy the outing, nothing more, nothing less. No guilt to contend with, no bossy, intrusive thoughts insisting calories be counted for lunch, that the distance and minutes spent walking be calculated to determine what, if anything, can be eaten for supper. Such intrusion plagued my mind when my children were young. One-on-one time with any child was impossible. The trip to the science show was pure 'grandson and me' time.

I had been working for 25 years towards recovery and had almost regained and rebuilt a sense of self, almost, when Lachlan was born five weeks prematurely. When the call came through, I had jumped in my car to drive two hours to the hospital.

On the way, unsettling thoughts crept in. If lucky enough to be photographed with this wee babe in my arms, would he think I looked fat and frumpish when he grew up? Perhaps I was not good enough to hold him anyway, perhaps I would not be good enough to play with him or mind him when his mummy, my daughter, went back to work or went out for dinner with his daddy.

As usual, thoughts raced ahead, grabbed uncertainty and amplified it. By the time I arrived at the hospital, my head was thumping. I hung back as the other grandparents excitedly went forward to peer into the crib containing the newest member of our family, and importantly the first member of the next generation.

But hey, my daughter was saying: 'Mum, would you like to hold Lachlan?' Me? Hold him? Oh joy on joy. Yes please! I glowed as I held the little bundle and looked down at the wee babe wrapped within. My heart wanted to burst. My sense of self surged.

Becoming a 'Grandma' introduced strong, secure and colourful threads of self into my psyche. The grandchildren weave the threads into a rich tapestry of connectedness, contentment and acceptance within. No room for the eating disorder.

Several months after Lachlan's birth, my daughter said, 'I want you to know, Mum, you are chief babysitter.' I cried. My daughter was telling me I was OK, accepted, worthwhile. Things I was unable to feel as a mother when she was a babe. I have not required antidepressant medication or therapy since the day Lachlan was born.

I am catching up on the things I have wanted to do for a long time. For instance, one day I got out my family photograph albums. Since age 11, when I got my first Brownie box camera, I have been the creator and keeper of pictorial records in my family. The albums number more than 50 and there are hundreds of pictures. Today, I leafed through each album, pausing, remembering, and occasionally slipping a picture out of its cover, and placing it in a special pile on my dining table as the first step in creating a book keepsake for my children. The task was easy enough, turning pages. But it was loaded with reminders of my pervasive eating disorder.

I stared in disbelief at pictures of each of my children with their annual birthday cakes. The children looked glum, even when about to huff and puff and blow out their candles. Their countenance was downright solemn. I calculated the years. Yes, I was in my thirties and forties, lost in the dark forest of my eating disorder, trying to find the way out. Counting calories, checking weights. Lost. At home and on family holidays, my illness ran amok. Binge, starve; good day, bad day. Moods see-sawing. Reflected in the faces. I felt desperately sad for my children and sad for me. We missed out on much time with each other. I tried to be a good mum, as best I could with the small amount of 'me' not consumed by the eating disorder, but my illness obviously had affected my children – and their dad. He looked glum, too. Not even saying 'smile for the camera' could raise a grin from anyone. The pictures told the story.

Oh hurry, hurry, through the albums to 2006. The year I regained me. Smiles: genuine smiles. My children are adults, becoming parents now; pictures of grandchildren begin to appear. Smiles, h-a-p-p-y and free. No eating disorder clouding, sabotaging relationships. I'm living in the moment ('Come on Grandma, it's time to play'). I squeeze through the tunnels in the playground, and whiz down the toddler's slide, granddaughter squealing with glee on my lap. At the seaside, throw shells in the waves. Plant carrot seeds in the garden. Blow bubbles, lots of bubbles, and chase them, too. Everyone is smiling. Including me. The pictures tell the story.

How lucky I am, that my children stayed by me, that their dad provided stability and security for them when I was too sick to do so. Today my children are my carers, recovery guides. Their children are the cheer squad.

Like the day I caught up with my grandchildren, upon returning to Australia from eating disorder conferences in the United States and book research in the UK. I coped with this 27-day absence from the important little people in my life, just! Shopping expeditions provided a distraction; browsing in bookshops and toyshops for gifts fostered happy thoughts, imagining the children's response on opening their surprises.

The children are a strategic part of my maintenance team; they are mini-carers, stress-relievers, hug-a-lots, happiness-givers, non-judges, and living-in-the-moment experts. ('Grandma, please help find this Lego part'; 'Grandma, you are my favourite when Mummy is at work'; 'Grandma, help me with this puzzle – sit on the FLOOR beside me, Grandma!'; 'I want you to come and read FIVE stories when I'm in bed tonight, and there is room for you to lie on the bed beside me, Grandma.')

I had been bossed around by eating disorders from the age of 11 until 55, and had spent years wondering who I really was. Who was I without the bossy eating disorder? My grandchildren have helped me work this out. It's simple really. To my parents and sister I was 'the one with the problems in the family' for so long that we became estranged. To my grandchildren, I am 'Grandma'. Their unconditional love makes all the difference. Together with three meals and three snacks a day, the grandchildren keep 'Ed' at bay. I am having fun, growing with them.

Do I have a take home message to share? Yes. Never give up on recovery.

# PART SIX

# Carers, Families and Friends

# 22

## Looking Out for Ed

### Signs of an eating disorder

Signs of an eating disorder are not necessarily visible. Mostly the symptoms are evident in thoughts and behaviours, and physical effects. They can be hard to spot. Weight may be associated with the physical symptoms, but an eating disorder is primarily a biologically based mental illness. Many people who have an eating disorder fit in the normal weight range – they are not necessarily underweight or overweight. Anorexia nervosa is not the most common but is the most serious eating disorder, with the highest death rate of any mental illness. It is the most visible eating disorder, while bulimia nervosa, binge eating disorder and Eating Disorder Not Otherwise Specified (EDNOS) are easier to hide. All eating disorders can be isolating for both the person developing the illness and their family.

#### Anorexia nervosa

Anorexia nervosa is characterized by self-starvation and excessive weight loss, or failure to make expected weight gains in children or younger adolescents. Worry signs: limiting food portions, cutting out groups of foods, avoiding family meals, exercising excessively, and becoming secretive. There may be anxiety or uneasiness about eating, or preoccupation with food, calories or exercise.

## Bulimia nervosa

Bulimia nervosa can be even more secretive, and any signs of bingeing and purging should be taken seriously. This illness is characterized by a cycle of bingeing and compensatory behaviours such as self-induced vomiting designed to undo or compensate for the effects of binge eating.

## Binge eating disorder

BED is characterized by recurrent binge eating without the regular use of compensatory measures to counter the binge eating.

## Eating Disorder Not Otherwise Specified

EDNOS is an eating disorder classification for a person who doesn't meet the criteria for anorexia nervosa or bulimia nervosa yet displays severe eating disordered symptoms. Examples are where the person meets the diagnostic criteria for anorexia nervosa and continues to have monthly menses or where the person engages in daily self-induced vomiting, with an absence of bingeing, and is not severely underweight.

# When Ed comes knocking

Eating disorders can confuse doctors as well as families and everyone agrees they can be difficult to understand.

We don't know that eating disorders can be prevented, but we can help to minimize triggers for young people who are vulnerable to developing the illness and for those people who are living with it. Mind you, the challenge is exacerbated because when you have an eating disorder you often do not understand that you are ill; therefore, why would you want to 'get well' by engaging in treatment? The illness is extremely manipulative:

the sufferer not only lacks insight into their condition, but also usually – in the early stages especially – likes it. The illness seems like a 'resident friend' in their mind. So why would they want to give up something with which they have developed a close bond? The illness can fool not only the sufferer, but also family, friends and doctors.

Ed rarely travels alone. Addictions and other co-morbid conditions, such as anxiety, depression, obsessive-compulsive disorder and Asperger syndrome, can complicate Ed treatment. Sometimes the person living with the illness does not realize they have an eating disorder until they hear someone speak about it and recognize the symptoms in themselves:

> 'I heard you speak about your eating disorder recovery and realize I have had what you had, at least since age 16, but the symptoms began about age 12. I have never really told anyone the truth about my anorexia and bulimia.
>
> I have been taking medication for 13 years for depression and anxiety. I had postnatal depression after the birth of both my boys, who are in their early twenties now. They have had a hard life, being raised by me.
>
> I often feel like I wished I wasn't here any more. I have told doctors and psychiatrists this but they have never picked up on my eating disorder symptoms. I think living in the country has not helped, as far as getting the help I have needed.
>
> Listening to your talk is the first time I have felt that someone knows what I'm going through.'
>
> *– Mother aged 48*

Then there is our culture – recovery is a confusing path when media and the fitness and weight-loss industries constantly confront and praise the very symptoms you are trying to overcome. Take calories, for instance. When you have an eating disorder you are often told not to count calories – 'Don't even think about them' – but they are listed on the label of almost every edible supermarket item; they are listed on menus in fast food outlets for all to see, and on restaurant menus. It's like holding a perpetual cigarette out to a person who is trying to give up smoking. As well, the media and marketing focus on only the slim being beautiful, which is cruelly confusing and confronting.

Another example is weight. When recovering from the eating disorder you are told to avoid the scales – don't think about weight, it is not important. But the media and the diet and fitness industries carry the message that weight largely determines our self-worth. The slim girl will get the most handsome boy. The slim girl will have the best sex. The slim girl will get the most lucrative job offer. The slim girl has her life under control. The slim girl will have the longest and happiest life, on and on the spiel goes. There is a spiel for boys, too. For them a six-pack abs makes all things possible.

The bombardment is so 'in your face' that people without eating disorders can get caught in this insidious web too. For people with an eating disorder, the negative impact is magnetic. The message that weight and food obsessions are normal aligns perfectly with the Ed 'voice'. So why would you want to give it up?

Then there is the cold, hard reality of finances – many health systems don't recognize the seriousness of eating disorders and fail to offer adequate treatment and care. Too often, tokenism is as good as it gets. This, together with a lack of social supports, can make recovery seem destined for the 'too hard' basket.

That's the down side.

Let's focus on the up side.

Research indicates that while eating disorders affect people of all ages, they almost always start to develop or emerge in childhood or adolescence. So, from this young age, we need to be on the lookout. Remember that prompt intervention provides best hope of a full recovery and, if you feel even a teeny bit concerned, check it out.

If you have a child in your care, educate yourself, especially about Maudsley Family Based Treatment, which is currently the most effective evidence-based treatment for children and adolescents with anorexia and increasingly with bulimia. In this treatment, the family consults with a therapist who helps parents take an active and positive role in restoring their child's health. The later stages of treatment focus on re-establishing independent eating and addressing concerns that interfere with resumption of healthy life and development. With good treatment and family support, there is every reason to be hopeful. If you are a parent or partner and feel concerned, make an appointment with a doctor, preferably one who has experience in treating eating disorders. Above all, trust your instinct and seek help straight away.

> 'If we had kick-started treatment with Family-Based Treatment, I believe our daughter's recovery prospects would have been much brighter. As it was, a medical professor said she was "driven" out of our family home.
>
> But our daughter says: "My illness drove me out of home."'
>
> *– Mother of 20-year-old*

Don't waste time on advice that you feel is going nowhere. Read as much as you can about evidence-based research outcomes so that you are in the best position to make a decision that is right for you. For time is the essence:

> 'During the past 12 months of living with our daughter's anorexia we have been given much advice and many opinions. If we had known at the outset what we know now we would have done things very differently:
>
> • We would have insisted that the general practitioner take our daughter's heart rate, temperature and blood pressure and also taken us seriously when we said that our daughter was unwell at our very first consultation.
>
> • At our second visit to the GP, I would have insisted on a referral to a paediatrician right then.

- I would have sought advice regarding medication for my daughter, who was experiencing co-morbid illnesses, from the word go.

- I would have sought a psychiatrist, psychologist or a person qualified to talk to my daughter about issues other than just food-related issues.

- When my daughter started to self-harm, I wish that I had screamed for someone to take me more seriously when we explained that we could not get her to stop this behaviour. At the same time I would have insisted that the doctors listen when explaining that our daughter did not have the capacity to know how to stop self-harming.

- I wish I had spoken to all the ambulance drivers and police officers in our area earlier and notified them of the condition of our daughter so they would know immediately when I called 000 [Australian emergency services] what they needed to prepare for.'

*– Mother of 13-year-old daughter with anorexia*

So if you are feeling worried about the child in your care, don't hesitate. Go along to your family doctor and explain you want the possibility of an eating disorder checked out. This is definitely one of those times when it is best to be safe than sorry. Early intervention can save years of heartbreak and suffering down the track. It can save a life. Act. Now.

Hold on to hope if your loved one is an adult who has been unable to access the right care or has relapsed. Persist in seeking support and new skills – for your loved one and yourself. There is evidence that recovery is possible at every age. Hug this knowledge, and never ever give up.

# When an eating disorder develops

Eating disorder symptoms are frightening, intrusive, antisocial, anxiety provoking and frustrating. The behaviours involved in controlling or limiting calorie intake or increasing calorie usage take many forms – the lengths to which the person with the eating disorder will go to avoid eating are often extraordinarily sneaky and very much out of character. The physical consequences – not always visible – are alarming and distressing. All semblance of normality disappears, social life evaporates, plans and lives are put on hold and interactions around food increasingly dominate – and test relationships.

Carers often have difficulty coping, and unfortunately can get trapped into a cycle of behaviour and emotional responses that can inadvertently perpetuate the illness. Professor Janet Treasure and her team at the Eating Disorder Unit of the Department of Psychiatry at King's College, London, have created a collaborative care skills training approach to help carers identify ways of reducing stress. Called the New Maudsley model, this approach is aimed at families of all sufferers. It is an additional treatment protocol, intended to reduce stress and empower carers by equipping them with a similar skill set to that encountered in an inpatient setting. The New Maudsley model is intended as an adjunct to treatment, as opposed to a treatment in its own right. For instance, animal analogies are used to show how different patterns of emotional response by parents and carers can help or hinder the recovery process. More information is available at http://thenewmaudsleyapproach.co.uk/FAQ.php.

Anorexia nervosa has a profound impact on loved ones both through the direct effect of the symptoms and indirectly by changing the person that families know and love. It can seem as though the mind of the loved one has been taken over by a bully who thrives on feeding misinformation. A family's reactions to this anorexic bully can change the course the illness takes.

'A psychotherapist provided guidance for me as well. I felt depressed, wondering if my behaviour in seeking a divorce had sparked my daughter's anorexia – but I think if I hadn't had a divorce, it would have been another trigger – I know this now but not then. I was running a business – I would walk around with a healthy slice of guilt and if things didn't improve I would get worried and depressed. As well as running a business I was trying to raise awareness of eating disorders at the girls' boarding school.'

*– Mother*

## Impact of anorexia nervosa on the sufferer

Brain starvation affects the deep inner self. Some aspects of personality are accentuated or new facets emerge. For example, at a low weight, behaviours often become ritualized and rule bound. Attention becomes focused on small details, particularly relating to food and weight, and it is hard to see beyond this to the bigger picture of life.

The person with the eating disorder may appear to be self-absorbed and unable to appreciate the plight of others. This is not because they are 'stuck up', or 'selfish' or 'unsympathetic', but because their illness is so demanding.

The cognitive resources that we use to make complex decisions and to understand the perspectives of other people are depleted in the mind of a person with an eating disorder. Communication and social interactions are less rewarding and the sufferer withdraws, becoming isolated. Furthermore, the loss of self-esteem and cognitive introspection that follows makes regulating emotions difficult. For some, frustration escalates into anger. Anxiety ascends to dread and fear becomes terror, sometimes manifesting as a panic attack. In others, there is too much inhibition of emotions. They may rely on their eating disorder to numb unpleasant emotions and therefore appear emotionally 'apathetic' or frozen; they may seem as if they 'don't care', but their illness has rendered them incapable of expressing their emotions, pleasant or unpleasant.

Parents, siblings and partners may think or fear the person that they have known and loved is lost or transformed 'forever' because of these changes in brain function. But don't despair.

# 23

# Helping the Recovery Process

## Causes of eating disorders

Locating the cause of an eating disorder remains an enigma, although recent research into genetics and neurobiology is starting to reveal why the illness develops in some people and not others. There is evidence of a strong genetic and biological component.

Several genetic factors play a role. For instance, certain temperament and personality traits, including childhood anxiety, are common in people who develop anorexia nervosa:

- A person who is more sensitive to punishment or threat. There may be many causes of this excess sensitivity, including genetic or even indirect difficulties experienced while in the womb or during childhood.

- An enhanced ability to perceive and analyse detail. This may be associated with a tendency to be focused and somewhat rigid.

- Stress (minor or major) can trigger onset, especially if it occurs during adolescence.

Many questions remain and misunderstandings abound. What is becoming clear is that reversal of this causal chain may not be possible, but treatment can be effective if it focuses on factors that cause the illness to persist, rather than those that have caused it.

## Message for parents, partners and close others

Banish any assumption that you are to blame for the eating disorder. Focus on the reality – you can be integral to the treatment process and ongoing recovery.

Refeeding is a vital first step. Whatever the eating disorder, the sufferer's brain needs nourishment to think clearly and rationally, and for their body to function best at a healthy weight. You can assist recovery by standing up to the illness on the sufferer's behalf until their weight is restored to a healthy level, and eating disorder behaviours diminish, and then remain vigilant.

You can help to interrupt the vicious circles that maintain the illness. Breaking through these traps will not be easy but the more people involved in this process, the better. You can gain skills to assist with the refeeding and to recognize and respond to behaviours which are traits of the illness rather than of your loved one.

> 'Early counselling with an eating disorder specialist who understood our daughter's illness would have helped – to be able to recognize how we were being manipulated and that the methods we were using to beat the illness were in fact 'preserving' it. I have attended a skills-based workshop recently which was very helpful but if I had had that from the beginning I may have not fallen into so many bad habits. I may actually have been encouraging my daughter to get better right from the start.'
>
> – *Carer of adult*

## Parents who have been carers offer these tips to help you and your family get through this difficult time

- Separate your child from the behaviours of the illness.

- Hug your other children every time you see them, because they are affected, too.

- Reach out to the eating disorder support organizations (see Appendix). It helps to share with others, and know that you are not alone in this struggle.

- Read as much as you can, to understand the illness: the support organizations recommend books to include on your shortlist.

- A sense of humour is still possible and essential.

- Find a therapist who is committed to evidence-based, family-based treatment and encourages parents to be primary caregivers for their child.

- Be wary of people working in the mental health or medical profession who, rather than suggest a collaborative treatment approach with you playing an integral role, indicate that your parental instincts count for nothing.

- Buckle in for a long ride: family therapy takes time, patience and determination; and most carers have to learn this through trial and error – look for caregiver workshops to help you gain the upper hand on Ed.

- Accept love and support from people you trust; avoid people who 'mean well' but make you feel terrible.

- Pamper yourself; this is possibly the hardest but also potentially the most rewarding challenge you will ever take on.

## A father shares wisdom gained as a carer (Anon)

Before we attended caregiver workshops my wife and I sometimes unknowingly hampered rather than helped our daughter's recovery by:

- Generally offering help, when we should have tried to let her sort things out herself or have said: 'If you want any help let us know' or by saying 'If I were you I would do this or say that.'

- Taking our daughter to visit friends or to parties by car, rather than letting her make her own way and own decisions on how to get there and how to get home. In hindsight it should have been a balance between the two.

- When we suggested things to eat or tried to get her to eat, saying the wrong words because we didn't understand what was going on in her mind or how to deal with the illness.

- Allowing her to continue to do a lot of homework at primary and secondary school stage because we thought it was best for her, when we should have encouraged her to take some time out. Then she would have had a better understanding of work–life balance when she went to university.

- When extended family asked my wife if our daughter had a boyfriend, my wife said our daughter 'spends most of her time studying and doesn't have time for boyfriends'. This was stating the true fact but our daughter understood it meant we didn't approve of her having a boyfriend and unbeknown to us decided not to go out with a young man who she liked. We would actually have loved for her to spend some social time away from studying. So there was misunderstanding and misinterpretation on both sides.

- If our daughter was upset, I would ask her what was wrong and want to try to solve the problem for her, rather than let her cry and try to sort it out herself; and only to tell her that if she couldn't sort it out, we were available to offer guidance.

My message to other dads is: try to stay calm at all times, seek help if required and try to keep an open mind because you might think you are doing the right things, when unbeknown to you they are the wrong things to do for someone suffering from an eating disorder. You might think you are helping but instead are making things worse.

## A mother shares her wisdom as a carer (Anon)

I felt absolutely devastated when I found my daughter had bulimia. She was about 18 and suffered from quantities of depression. My heart plummeted. Someone had told me this illness lasted for years.

My daughter certainly was depressed, holed up in her room for days on end, but eventually her illness brought about a turning point in each of our lives, and in our relationship.

She was so depressed she tried to commit suicide – thankfully that didn't work. After that attempt – she had been having outpatient therapy – she was transferred to a private clinic. I was to learn that my habit of taking all responsibility from my daughter was preventing her from moving on.

Her ability to develop and mature was being hampered because I wouldn't let go – I would help her find a job, find a flat – my helping was obsessive – anything she said, I would do better – she needed to get away from my smothering attitude and take responsibility for her own attitude and actions. Like, if that meant she would not have a job for years, then that would be her problem.

I had to learn to be a parent and set boundaries that were healthy. This was one of most important things that happened to our family as a result of my daughter's eating disorder.

The crunch came when eventually the clinic forbade my daughter to see me. Three or four years had passed since her bulimia became known. It was shortly after her twenty-first birthday. She wrote a letter saying: 'Mum, I love you very much but I want you out of my life.'

She said: 'I don't want to see you until we sort this out.'

Professor Janet Treasure calls my habit 'over-caring'. I was absolutely devastated and came very close to letting depression get the better of me as I dealt with this issue. I couldn't bear to be alone and I am normally a great loner. I would not stop talking and spent a massive time in tears. I couldn't believe someone I loved and in whom I had invested years of my life was telling me to push off and stay away.

In a way I am the lucky one because what happened next was that the leaders of the carer group I was attending took me aside and said: 'You need to consider your own treatment'.

I respected their advice, accepted my behaviour was not helping and I enrolled in the 12-step programme for over-caring. The guidance in Janet's book (*Skills-based Learning for Caring for a Loved One with an Eating Disorder*) is very similar to the treatment I underwent. It revolutionized both my daughter's recovery and my whole life. With my changes in attitude and behaviour, my daughter quickly got into recovery.

I learnt carers have a need to recognize and be open to accepting that looking after someone with a mental health problem is different to looking after someone with a normal medical illness.

I have since met many parents who are over-smothering. They feel like doing everything. But helping a child recover from an eating disorder is about setting and recognizing the boundaries and being open to being told how to do things. I think a lot of carers find it difficult to accept what they are told; perhaps due to how they are told. It is a leap of faith. When you learn what you have to do – the next step is putting it into practice and this is definitely a leap of faith.

## Caring for the carer – when mothers have eating disorders

An adult woman who has children, and is battling an eating disorder, is often very good at feeding her family but not herself. She is conscious of not providing a good role model for her children, and this adds to her sense of guilt and unworthiness. Meal times provide a multitude of challenges. Unlike a child, who is still in the parents' overall care, an adult can insist that they are independent and don't need to take any notice of you. It is harder still when the person with the ED is sole carer in the house, and is struggling with the line that food is non-negotiable. It can help immensely to have someone else take on the responsibility for food preparation.

> 'I'm struggling with knowing I need to eat, but also being responsible for having to feed everyone in the family, including myself. The "including myself" often becomes too challenging, so I give up. I talk myself out of it! My husband is very supportive, but he also works very long hours, so it does not seem reasonable to expect him to come home and then cook for me – like it or not, being a mother, this is my job ☺'
>
> *– Mother aged 37*

## Insight as an adult with an eating disorder (June Alexander)

As a wife and mother in the 1970s, the same tussle of thoughts preceded every meal – I had not been told about the importance of eating three meals and three snacks a day and as the main caregiver in the family, I always put the needs of others first.

Secretly, though, I yearned to be in a confined and restricted situation, where meals would be provided at regular times. For instance, for the few days in hospital after the birth of a child, or after an operation, I was able to eat 'normally'. In such a controlled environment I could eat the meals, as someone else had prepared them, and they would be served on a tray. Somehow, this was acceptable as I was not responsible for deciding what food would be on my plate. Having been allocated a certain amount, I could eat it without feeling overridden with guilt. The restricting and bingeing symptoms of my eating disorder would fall away and I would think: 'This must be what it is like to be NORMAL' and would fastidiously plan to continue eating three meals a day when I returned home.

Of course, when I returned home, without support structures in place, the eating disorder behaviours screamed and shouted, sabotaged the vulnerable me, and resumed their domination.

At home, I fed and prolonged my illness behaviours. I needed a recovery guide in my kitchen, to take charge in preparation, serving and eating of the meals. I needed a guide to confront my illness until I was strong enough (had regained sufficient of my identity) to confront it myself. But the knowledge was not around then.

For years I chose, at some inner level, to live a part-life with my illness – even though I knew it was not good for me. Hanging on to the illness seemed less terrifying than confronting it and it was easy to pretend I didn't have time to do so (that would be selfish). Others needed me. This meant I often remained in unsuitable and chaotic situations, much to the despair of family, friends and colleagues, who had no idea of my torment within.

Recovery from an eating disorder is initially a full time job in itself. Adult women – in their roles as carers for young children or ageing parents or as professionals in demanding careers, are easily persuaded by the eating disorder thoughts to give only token attention to the recovery challenge. Recovery requires us to put ourselves first. The illness 'voice' will always try to convince us to put ourselves last so that it can maintain its hold. Listening to that 'voice' destines us for a part-life whereby we may go through the motions of life, but never become fully engaged.

Day after day I created nourishing dishes for husband and children and, while they tucked into their hearty and balanced meal, loaded my plate with green and yellow vegetables (so that it seemed a lot). Or if I had been upset and binged, I would pretend I had eaten already, and eat nothing at all. My body missed out on a lot of essential nutrition.

A recovery guide at meal times would have helped recovery immensely – someone to confront Ed on my behalf until I was recovered sufficiently to eat the same meals as everyone else.

## When you are your own carer – strategies for meal times

- Confide in someone you trust – a parent, sibling, friend or partner – and ask them to be your meal recovery guide. Honesty is imperative. Write down the meal times, and what you will eat for each meal. Share this menu with your meal recovery guide each night, for the next day, and report on your progress.

- No avoiding your meals, OK? Even if you have binged on ten packets of cookies. Eat your next meal. You will be amazed at how you gradually lose the urge to eat ten packets of cookies or two litres of ice cream. Why? Because you are not going to punish yourself with starvation any more. You are breaking the 'feast and famine' cycle. Remember, food is our medicine.

- Three meals a day are ESSENTIAL to breaking free of Ed. Do not miss one meal or snack!

- Choose a recovery guide, or several, who can be with you 24/7 to jump-start the refeeding process. Your partner could take medical leave from their job for a few weeks, or another family member or friend could come and visit.

- When you need to resume work or go home, invite other relatives, neighbours and friends over to help with some meals. Take steps to guard against relapse.

- If you have children, they could go and stay with their grandparent or another relative for a week or so, to give you a break and allow you to fully focus on recovery.

- With your recovery guide, plan meals in advance, writing down exact foods and quantities that you will eat (non-negotiable).

- Ideally, and to deny the eating disorder's crafty knack of convincing you to have a smaller serving, or to leave food on your plate, arrange with your recovery guide to have them or someone else sit with you for every meal until your will is stronger than Ed's voice. If that is not possible, another option is to have a phone or Skype conversation with your recovery guide while you are eating the meal. Let your support team share the responsibility. They can help to weaken Ed's resolve by diverting your thoughts off the food and on to far more interesting topics.

- Be honest with yourself (as distinct from your illness). You will require the recovery guide's assistance until you have regained sufficient 'self' to be able to ignore the illness thoughts.

- If suffering with bulimia, have someone sit with or communicate with you for at least half an hour after each meal.

- If you go to work or are studying, confide in a trusted colleague or friend and ask them to sit with you while eating your lunch. Text messages from the recovery guide can provide encouragement and keep you accountable for the eating of snacks.

- Several evidence-based treatments offer support – the Maudsley Family Based Treatment approach is showing promise in being adaptable for young adults, and there are special programmes for couples.

- There will be feelings to sort, and skills to learn, as you rebuild your identity free of Ed. Getting the three meals and three snacks established as your daily 'medicine' provides the best foundation on which to recover your life and forge full throttle on the road ahead.

# PART SEVEN
## Myths and Truths

# 24

## Focus on the Facts

Eating disorder myths permeate every aspect of the illness. Myths are dangerous. They discourage people who develop the illness and their families from recognizing the signs and symptoms and seeking appropriate and prompt treatment. Even health professionals sometimes dismiss signs and symptoms and say 'Come back again in six weeks if you still feel concerned.' Education and awareness are the strongest antidotes for misinformation. A better understanding of eating disorders in families, communities and among media and healthcare providers will give promise of a much brighter outcome. It's time to extinguish the misconceptions and put the record straight.

The challenge is huge. Eating disorder awareness runs the risk of being over-run and lost in the whirl created by multinational companies bent on encouraging and exploiting the socio-cultural obsession with body image. Thousands of people are living part lives, and families are living part lives, because of eating disorders. Many are feeling trapped and isolated. Too many have lost their lives.

This chapter will explain how misinterpretation of the language of eating disorders has fuelled misconceptions and strengthened rather than healed the illness. Eating disorders can be successfully treated. If the opportunity for early intervention is missed, long and strenuous efforts are required to re-establish good health and re-engage in life. There is no quick solution. Recovery comes slowly – often over several or many years – and with occasional relapses, but the good news is that with the right treatment, a full sense of self can be regained – at every age.

## Who gets an eating disorder?

**Myth: Only young girls and adolescent females suffer from eating disorders.**

Truth: Many eating disorders begin during childhood and adolescence, but boys as well as girls – and adults – can develop an eating disorder. Many adults suffer from eating disorders because they were not treated successfully when they were young, or because they have suffered a relapse.

**Myth: Eating disorders are a women's illness.**

Truth: Eating disorders occur in males. The disorders are believed to be more common than reflected in statistics because of under-diagnosis. Incidence in males may be under-reported because females are more likely to seek help, and health practitioners are more likely to consider an eating disorder diagnosis in females. Whereas females are more likely to focus on weight loss, males are more likely to focus on muscle mass. Males may take longer than females to seek professional help and treatment due to the stigma associated with having what they or others wrongly perceive to be 'a female disorder'.

**Myth: Eating disorders predominantly affect girls from affluent or privileged families and those from western cultures where the 'ideal beauty' involves being thin and toned.**

Truth: People develop eating disorders regardless of ethnicity, colour or social class.

**Myth: People who get eating disorders simply have nothing better to do with their time and would 'get over it' if they got a hobby.**
Truth: While some people find employment or hobbies can be beneficial to their recovery, the illness does not develop due to boredom. An eating disorder is an illness of the brain just as juvenile diabetes is an illness of the pancreas. People don't develop diabetes because they are bored.

**Myth: People who want attention adopt eating disorder behaviours.**
Truth: During a person's illness prior to diagnosis and throughout their treatment and recovery they may appear to need and seek attention. This attention, however, is sought for reassurance of their self-worth, not because they are self-centred. Often the sufferer feels unworthy of help or love, and in the absence of internal resilience skills will look externally for this validation. It is a sign that you might need to provide extra support rather than withdraw it.

**Myth: Men who suffer from eating disorders tend to be gay.**
Truth: Sexual orientation has no correlation with developing an eating disorder.

**Myth: People who are normal or overweight cannot have eating disorders.**
Truth: Yes, they can. Eating disorders are not solely identified by size and weight. Many other factors must be considered. People with bulimia tend to be an average, or even above average, weight. People with binge eating disorder may be overweight but not necessarily so, while people with anorexia are not always underweight.

**Myth: Children under age 15 are too young to have an eating disorder.**
Truth: Eating disorders rarely begin before puberty but have been diagnosed in children as young as seven years of age. Precursor behaviours often are not recognized until middle to

late adolescence. The average age at onset for anorexia is 17 years. Bulimia is usually diagnosed in mid-to-late adolescence or early twenties, although some people do not seek treatment until aged in their thirties or forties – often because they feel ashamed of their 'secret' and feel a need to guard it.

## Anorexia nervosa

**Myth: You can always tell someone is suffering anorexia by their appearance – they are thin and don't eat.**
Truth: Not all people with anorexia look like the extreme cases that have been shown in the media. You can have anorexia, be of normal weight and appear physically fit. Just because someone does not look emaciated, does not mean they are not suffering anorexia, or that their health is not in danger.

**Myth: People with anorexia do not eat candy, chocolate or other sweet foods.**
Truth: Many people with anorexia avoid rich, sugary foods, but prior to recovery some may devote their entire, meagre daily allowance of calories to one small chocolate bar, for example. It depends what you get 'stuck' on – it can be very scary, changing to a different food.

**Myth: People with anorexia do not binge or purge.**
Truth: Some people develop a sub-type of anorexia whereby they will occasionally binge and purge. Some sufferers become so fearful of any food or drink that they will purge whatever they consume, including water.

**Myth: Achieving normal weight means the anorexia is cured.**
Truth: Regular, balanced nutrition, weight recovery and maintenance is essential to enable a person with anorexia to participate meaningfully in further treatment – such as attending to any unaddressed emotional issues – to help get their life back on track. Achievement of a normal weight marks the first step in

the recovery process – it does not alone signify a cure, because eating disorders are complex medical and psychiatric illnesses.

**Myth: Once you develop anorexia, you have anorexia forever.**
Truth: Recovery statistics are optimistic, especially when children and adolescents have access to early intervention with family-based treatments (FBT), also known as the Maudsley approach.

**Myth: Anorexia is the only serious eating disorder.**
Truth: The death rate from anorexia is reported to be the highest among all psychiatric illnesses. But other eating disorders can be life threatening, too. All can have damaging physical and psychological consequences.

**Myth: A person with anorexia never eats.**
Truth: Most people with anorexia do eat; however, they tend to eat smaller portions, low-calorie foods, or certain food combinations that they become set on.

Total cessation or low intake of food or liquid requires urgent medical attention.

# Bulimia nervosa

**Myth: Bulimia is a good way to lose weight.**
Truth: Bulimia is an ineffective and dangerous weight control method. Over time, people with bulimia may gain weight.

**Myth: People who have bulimia always consume huge amounts of calories in one sitting and throw up immediately afterward.**
Truth: Binges can vary in size and a person does not need to vomit to have bulimia.

**Myth: Purging will help lose weight.**
Truth: Purging does not rid the body of ingested food. Half of what is consumed during a binge typically remains in the body after self-induced vomiting. Laxatives result in weight loss through

fluids/water and the effect is temporary. For these reasons, many people with bulimia are average or above average weight.

**Myth: Purging is only throwing up.**
Truth: Purging involves the removal of contents in the stomach or bowels, or elimination of calories through excessive exercise. A person with bulimia purges to compensate for excessive food intake. Methods of purging include vomiting, enemas and laxative and insulin abuse. Each of these behaviours can endanger health. Purging by throwing up also can affect the teeth and oesophagus because of the acidity of purged contents.

**Myth: A person cannot die from bulimia.**
Truth: Although the death rate from bulimia is lower than that from anorexia, a person with bulimia can be at high risk for death because of purging and its impact on the heart and electrolyte imbalances. Laxative use and excessive exercise can increase risk of death in people who suffer bulimia.

**Myth: All people with bulimia purge by self-induced vomiting.**
Truth: People who develop bulimia typically binge and purge, but not everyone tries to rid themselves of the calories they have consumed by self-induced vomiting. Some over-exercise, fast, or use diuretics and laxatives.

**Myth: Laxatives prevent calorie absorption.**
Truth: Many people with eating disorders, especially those with bulimia, use laxatives. These laxatives are used in an attempt to quickly rid the body of food before calories are absorbed. However, laxatives assist only in draining the body of its necessary fluids and in causing colon problems.

# Binge eating disorder

**Myth: 'It's hopeless, I'm hopeless!' You cannot stop bingeing.**
Truth: You can recover from binge eating disorder (BED).

**Myth: BED is no different to bulimia.**
Truth: BED is a separate and distinct eating disorder from bulimia. BED is characterized by recurrent binge eating episodes during which a person feels a loss of control and strong feelings of embarrassment and guilt, similar to bulimia. But unlike bulimia, purging behaviour such as vomiting or laxatives, excessive exercise or fasting, does not follow BED binge eating episodes.

**Myth: Everyone who has BED must be fat.**
Truth: Not so. Some people who suffer BED are not overweight or obese but are deeply concerned about their body shape, size or weight. Some people with BED are underweight.

**Myth: Binge eating isn't a real disorder. It's about being weak and out of control – an excuse to keep eating.**
Truth: BED is a real disorder listed (along with anorexia and bulimia) for inclusion in the *Diagnostic and Statistical Manual of Mental Disorders* (DSM-V), the 'bible' of mental illness.

**Myth: Binge eaters have no willpower.**
Truth: Many binge eaters are highly successful people with plenty of drive and determination. Remember, BED is an illness, just like cancer or diabetes is an illness. The illness does not develop because of lack of willpower.

**Myth: Binge eaters should just go on a diet.**
Truth: Dieting can't 'cure' binge eating disorder. Traditional calorie-restriction diets can actually trigger binges, even in people who don't have binge eating disorder.

**Myth: Binge eating is a female thing.**
Truth: Eating disorders are more common in women, but men suffer too. We don't know exact figures as many suffer silently.

**Myth: People with BED just don't know when to stop eating.**
Truth: It's more serious than that. The BED illness compels you to keep going beyond the point when you feel comfortably full – even if the food is burnt, spoiled, dropped on the floor or on the way to the rubbish bin.

**Myth: Children don't develop BED.**
Truth: BED behaviour has been seen in children as young as six. A parent who suspects a child is sneaking food, hiding food or experiencing a loss of control around food should consult an eating disorder expert.

**Myth: Recovery means avoiding 'trigger foods' forever.**
Truth: Sugary, fatty or carbohydrate-rich foods can trigger binge eating in some people, but recovery includes education on the importance of nourishing and satisfying the body.

**Myth: Surgery is the key to recovery.**
Truth: Gastric bypass and other forms of weight-loss (bariatric) surgery may eliminate some problems caused by obesity. But the disorder that causes people to binge eat may remain. After weight-loss surgery, some former binge eaters can't eat as much food as they once did. Some develop addictive behaviours such as drinking or compulsive shopping. More research is needed to determine the all-round efficacy of bariatric surgery for BED.

# Eating disorders other than anorexia, bulimia and binge eating disorder

**Myth: You cannot have more than one eating disorder.**
Truth: You can have more than one eating disorder. People who have symptoms of more than one type of eating disorder, or who

do not fit all the criteria for one, may be classified as suffering an Eating Disorder Not Otherwise Specified (EDNOS).

**Myth: A diagnosis of EDNOS means you don't really have an eating disorder.**
Truth: EDNOS is a diagnosed eating disorder category. Like other defined eating disorders, EDNOS has serious health risks. As well, sufferers may feel a failure because, in their view, they aren't good enough to be diagnosed with (typically) anorexia – when your self-esteem is already low, any perceived failure compounds the feelings of inadequacy.

# Recovery

**Myth: Eating disorders are not life threatening.**
Truth: Every eating disorder carries a real threat of being potentially life threatening if not treated in time or with proper care.

**Myth: Eating disorders are primarily about food.**
Truth: 'Just eat' might be your intuitive response to someone who refuses to eat – or to someone who is bingeing you might say: 'For goodness sake, just stop eating.' But these comments are not helpful when you have an eating disorder. Eating disorders are an illness. Willpower alone is not sufficient to survive and recover from a heart attack; and the same applies to an eating disorder. Expert help is required.

**Myth: Eating disorders are 'untreatable'.**
Truth: This myth contributes to a sense of hopelessness that sometimes pervades people with an eating disorder – not just in the family or community, but also among health professionals. Early intervention with evidence-based treatment is associated with better outcomes, and people are known to recover at every age. It is important to remain hopeful and to persist in recovery efforts. Recovery can take months or years, but most people eventually recover.

**Myth: For FBT to be successful, both parents need to live with the sufferer.**
Truth: FBT can work perfectly well with a single parent family or other family structures. Marital status is not a prerequisite for success.

**Myth: You can never fully recover from an eating disorder.**
Truth: Recovery can take a long time, but with hard work and the proper treatment, you can fully recover from your eating disorder. Early intervention with evidence-based treatment offers best hope for early recovery but there is hope at all ages and stages.

**Myth: You have to 'want' to get better to recover from an eating disorder.**
Truth: It is natural to want to get well when you are sick, but people with anorexia, for instance, are likely to be incapable of understanding that they are ill. They may give every indication that they don't want to get well, and carers and the treatment team may feel frustrated. While some sufferers, with difficulty, may be able to see past their illness and take steps towards recovery, this is not possible for many. Many sufferers are incapable of recognizing that they are ill or understanding the severity of their symptoms – particularly during acute stages of their illness. Waiting for someone to 'want to get better' can delay treatment and allow the sufferer's physical condition to deteriorate and their ED to become further entrenched. With an eating disorder, particularly in the early stages when the body is undernourished, a person can be incapable of understanding they are not well (anosognosia); so what other people are saying seems stupid. Eating disorders can cause immense emotional and physical barriers to recovery. Therefore loved ones, carers and treatment providers need to fight the illness on the sufferer's behalf until they recover sufficiently to appreciate that they are indeed ill. At this point the sufferer can be encouraged and assisted in becoming proactive in achieving recovery.

# Body image

**Myth: Being thin equates to happiness.**
Truth: People with anorexia nervosa learn that happiness does not automatically follow weight loss. A goal weight is reached and there is pressure to meet another goal weight, and another. A number on scales is not a prerequisite for happiness. Happiness is possible regardless of weight or circumstances.

**Myth: People who are normal weight or overweight cannot have eating disorders.**
Truth: Yes, they can. Eating disorders are not determined solely by the size and weight of a person.

**Myth: Going without one meal each day is one way to lose weight and improve health.**
Truth: Eating three meals a day may actually help to prevent obesity. Skipping a meal increases the likelihood of overeating or binge eating later in the day. Three meals and three snacks a day is important 'medicine' for everyone.

**Myth: Our culture and society has always valued thinness as a sign of beauty. It will never change.**
Truth: Standards of beauty vary from culture to culture and change over time. Remember, eating disorders occur in all body sizes.

**Myth: Eating disorders are only about how the person looks.**
Truth: Eating disorders are biologically based mental illnesses.

**Myth: Appearance is a sure way to detect an eating disorder.**
Truth: An eating disorder cannot be determined by appearance alone; likewise appearance alone cannot determine if recovery is complete. People with an eating disorder can become very effective at hiding the signs and symptoms. Eating disorders can be undetected for months, years, or a lifetime.

# Weight-loss dieting

**Myth: Fat-free eating is healthy eating.**
Truth: Some fat and oils are needed for good health. Moderate, balanced eating is healthy eating. When eaten in moderation, there are no bad foods.

**Myth: Weight-loss dieting achieves permanent weight control.**
Truth: Dieting and food restriction are the least effective way to lose weight. 'Yo-yo' dieting, where weight is taken off, put on, taken off, often leads to higher rather than lower weight in the long term.

**Myth: With a sensible diet and a strong commitment, everyone can become and remain thin.**
Truth: People come in all shapes and sizes, and body size depends on more than diet and commitment – it also depends on genetics.

**Myth: Vomiting or using laxatives gets rid of the calories consumed by eating.**
Truth: Even when vomiting takes place immediately after eating, it does not get rid of all calories consumed. Similarly, laxatives don't prevent calories being absorbed. Repeated vomiting and laxative abuse can cause serious health problems and even death.

**Myth: Fad dieting is a good way to lose weight.**
Truth: Fad diets, or any short-term weight loss strategy, might work initially, but in the long term, almost always lead to weight gain. This is because dieting slows down the body's metabolism making it harder to burn off calories consumed. Dieting also increases preoccupation with food and craving, to the point where more food may be eaten than if not dieting.

**Myth: Dieting is normal adolescent behaviour and everyone grows out of it.**
Truth: Significant weight gain is a normal part of adolescent growth and development. Frequent or extreme dieting can be a

risk factor for developing an eating disorder – especially for young people with family histories of eating disorders and depression, anxiety, or obsessive-compulsive disorder. It's not worth the risk.

**Myth: If your parents are obese, your genetic make-up may prevent you from being lean and fit.**
Truth: Obesity tends to run from one generation to the next. Whatever your genetic make-up, you will be healthier if you enjoy a lifestyle that includes a good balanced diet and some regular exercise.

**Myth: Being the 'ideal weight' for height and age means you are healthy.**
Truth: 'Ideal weights' are simply statistical averages of large populations and do not give meaningful information about an individual's ideal weight. Being at a weight that is healthy for you is more important than weighing an 'ideal number'.

**Myth: The media are to blame for the prevalence of eating disorders.**
Truth: Media messages do not cause eating disorders. Messages that promote thinness as an asset can be triggering for people vulnerable to developing an eating disorder, and for people trying to recover from an eating disorder.

**Myth: Eating disorders are just a phase.**
Truth: Eating disorders are not phases, but serious biologically based mental disorders.

**Myth: Vitamins and supplements can replace food.**
Truth: No, they can't. Calories, protein and fat as well as vitamins and minerals are needed in a healthy diet. You need food (three meals and three snacks a day).

**Myth: She can't have an eating disorder; she eats with us every day.**
Truth: Eating disorders can cause secretive, deceptive behaviour – which may go unnoticed by other family members for years. You

may eat or go through the motions of eating with your family, and then purge by vomiting or taking laxatives later.

## Getting help

**Myth: To have an eating disorder you must be emaciated. Seeking help before then is wasting the doctor's time.**
Truth: Most people with eating disorders do not get dangerously underweight. The false belief that you are only truly ill if abnormally thin compounds misconceptions about eating disorders. Thoughts that you are not yet 'thin enough' can trigger self-destructive ED behaviours. Don't delay – if feeling concerned, seek help today.

**Myth: Eating disorders are an attempt to seek attention.**
Truth: The causes of eating disorders are complex and include biological, behavioural, emotional, psychological, interpersonal and social factors. Attention seeking does not rate a mention.

**Myth: Eating disorders are not an illness.**
Truth: Eating disorders are a complex illness, often requiring both medical and psychiatric care over months or years. They can co-occur with other mental illness such as major depression, Asperger syndrome, anxiety and obsessive-compulsive disorder.

**Myth: Eating disorders are rare.**
Truth: Increased rates of anorexia nervosa, bulimia nervosa and binge eating disorder are being reported in many countries. This may be due to more awareness, as many people have been suffering in silence for years – often because they feel ashamed, are not aware they have a diagnosable illness, and don't know where to get help.

## Eating disorders as a choice

**Myth: Eating disorders are all about food.**
Truth: The causes of eating disorders are not well understood. Issues with food and weight are just some of the more obvious symptoms of these complex, biologically based mental illnesses.

**Myth: Eating disorders are an illness of choice.**
Truth: Eating disorders are a biologically based mental illness, and no one chooses to have an eating disorder. Recovering from the disease is more complicated than simply making healthy lifestyle choices.

**Myth: Eating disorders aren't serious illnesses.**
Truth: The mortality rates associated with eating disorders are higher than any other mental illness, including depression, bipolar disorder and schizophrenia. Anorexia, characterized by inability to maintain a healthy body weight and by an obsessive fear of gaining weight, has the highest incidence of deaths of all eating disorders.

**Myth: People with eating disorders are 'dying to be thin'.**
Truth: Eating disorder patients often believe they must lose weight. Their attitude is understandable for they are seriously mentally ill. The desire to be thin is a symptom of their illness. But inferences that people with the illness are choosing or dying to be thin are dangerously wrong.

**Myth: Eating disorders are about appearance and beauty.**
Truth: Eating disorders are a biologically based mental illness and have little to do with appearance or beauty. This is indicated by the continuation of the illness long after the initial 'target' weight and 'normal appearance' is achieved.

## Families

**Myth: Dysfunctional families cause eating disorders.**

Truth: Families are not a cause of the illness, but rather an integral part of eating disorders recovery. While families don't cause eating disorders, these illnesses have been shown to run in families. The risk of developing an eating disorder is largely genetic. A person with a mother or sister who has, or has had, the illness is more likely than the general population to also develop the disease. An eating disorder can be triggered in people with a latent genetic vulnerability by a precipitating event, such as a change in diet, trauma or major life change.

**Myth: Parental involvement in an adolescent's life is intrusive and violates privacy and independence. Insisting that they eat their meals is insulting – it's like treating them like a baby.**

Truth: Children and adolescents with malnourished brains are incapable of rational, clear perceptions and the good judgement required for self-care and effective problem solving. To recover, they need someone to step in and take charge until they are capable of assuming control of themselves. When parents become involved in treatment with the healthcare team, the child typically, deep down, feels relieved that their secret is out so that they can get help. Research shows that, for most cases, family-based therapy is more effective than individual treatment for children living at home who have been diagnosed with anorexia for less than three years.

**Myth: People who adopt eating disorder behaviours do this to hurt their family and friends.**

Truth: People with eating disorders do not choose to have the illness. They are usually very upset when they know the people around them are worried or hurt by their eating disorder.

**Myth: The root cause of an eating disorder is an inability to be angry with one's mother.**
Truth: An eating disorder is a problem with brain function exacerbated by and maintained by eating behaviours. What a mother does or does not do, or does not understand, is relevant, but not for the reason implied here. If a family has been held at bay, lied to and frightened by the illness behaviours and their concern has been hostilely and repeatedly rejected, the parents are likely to be confused and may withdraw. Parents and partners need to understand that an eating disorder is a treatable mental illness and that symptoms, which are similar between patients, are alleviated with improved nutrition and symptom intervention.

## Symptoms and signs

**Myth: There is no such thing as too much exercise.**
Truth: Exercising excessively, without sufficient caloric absorption, can be harmful for physical, mental and emotional health.

**Myth: Adolescents are naturally non-communicative, rude, moody and withdrawn as part of the normal process of separation from the family as they head toward adulthood.**
Truth: If dysfunctional attitudes and behaviours in a child are accepted as the norm or a rite of passage, parents run the risk of missing important warning signs of eating disorders. Detection of early warning signs is the key to prevention and prompt intervention. Parents' instincts concerning their child are strong – if you are worried, seek help.

# Appendix

# Eating Disorder Advocacy and Support Organizations

**Parent-led or focused organization

## International

**Academy for Eating Disorders (AED)**
*www.aedweb.org*

**Eating Disorder Mentoring (EDM)**
*www.eatingdisordermentoring.org*

**Families Empowered and Supporting Treatment of Eating Disorders (F.E.A.S.T.)****
*www.feast-ed.org*

**International Association of Eating Disorder Professionals (IAEDP)**
*www.iaedp.com*

## Australia

**Australia and New Zealand Academy for Eating Disorders**
*www.anzaed.org.au*

**National Eating Disorders Collaboration**
*www.nedc.com.au*

**Victorian Centre of Excellence in Eating Disorders**
*www.ceed.org.au*

## Canada

**Bulimia Anorexia Nervosa Association**
*www.bana.ca*

**Danielle's Place (Burlington)**
*www.daniellesplace.org*

**Looking Glass Foundation\*\***
*www.lookingglassbc.com*

**NEDIC (National Eating Disorder Information Centre)**
*www.nedic.ca*

## Ireland

**Eating Disorder Resource Centre of Ireland**
*www.eatingdisorders.ie*

**ED Contact\*\***
*www.edcontact.com*

## New Zealand

**Eating Disorders Association of New Zealand (EDANZ)\*\***
*www.ed.org.nz*

## United Kingdom

**Anorexia and Bulimia Care**
*www.anorexiabulimiacare.org.uk*

**Anorexia Carers\*\***
*www.anorexiacarers.co.uk*

**Beat (Beating Eating Disorders)**
*www.b-eat.co.uk*

**The New Maudsley Approach**
*http://thenewmaudsleyapproach.co.uk/FAQ.php*

# United States

**A Chance to Heal\*\***
*http://achancetoheal.org*

**Alliance for Eating Disorders Awareness**
*www.allianceforeatingdisorders.com*

**Amy Helpenstell Foundation**
*amyhelpenstell.org*

**Amy's Gift**
*www.trinityqc.com/Medical-Services/-Medical-Services-eatingdisorders.aspx*

**ANAD: National Association of Anorexia Nervosa and Associated Disorders**
*www.anad.org*

**Andrea's Voice\*\***
*www.andreasvoice.org*

**Anna Westin Foundation\*\***
*www.annawestinfoundation.org*

**Binge Eating Disorder Association (BEDA)**
*www.bedaonline.com/aboutus.html*

**Eating for Life Alliance**
*www.eatingforlife.org*

**The Elisa Project**
*www.theelisaproject.org*

**Gurze Books**
*www.bulimia.com*

**Hope Network\*\***
*http://hopenetwork.info*

**Maudsley Parents\*\***
*www.maudsleyparents.org*

**MentorConnect**
*www.key-to-life.com/mentorconnect*

**Multiservice Eating Disorders Association (MEDA)**
*www.medainc.org*

**The National Association for Males With Eating Disorders (NAMED)**
*www.namedinc.org*

**National Eating Disorders Association**
*www.nationaleatingdisorders.org*

**NEDA network members**
*www.nationaleatingdisorders.org/about-us/neda-network.php#members*

**Ophelia's Place, Inc.\*\***
*http://opheliasplace.org*

**Proud2bme – online community created for and by teens**
*http://proud2bme.org and www.proud2bme.nl*

This list of organizations is largely sourced from http://feast-ed.org/LocalSupport/AdvocacyandSupportOrganizations.aspx

# Afterword

Eating disorders thrive on secrecy, take root in hiding, and overwhelm people by stealth. When one person in the family develops the condition, everyone feels the effects and those effects are devastating.

Every time someone speaks up, speaks out and shines a light on an eating disorder, the deadly grip of this most challenging illness is weakened. June Alexander and Cate Sangster have beamed that light with their compilation of many views, so much hard-won insight.

Giving a voice to people who have lived experience of an eating disorder and their families gives hope to all those many, many others who find themselves still seeking recovery and restoration.

Eating disorders are complex, and leading researchers worldwide are working to understand the causes and determine effective treatments. The answers are not all known yet. It isn't even known if we are talking about one illness with many different variations or many different illnesses.

What is known is that, regardless of diagnosis, recovery is possible, health can be regained, potential can be fulfilled and eating disorders can be beaten.

So much of an eating disorder goes against the grain of common sense. Why can't the person with the illness just eat – or stop overeating? Don't they know how unattractive it is to look that way? How can anyone believe they are fat when their bones are plainly visible for all to see? It's not logical. It's hard to believe that someone who looks emaciated and hasn't eaten for ages is being honest with you when they say they are completely full after one mouthful of food.

The confusion is compounded by the person with the eating disorder being typically very logical, fluent and persuasive, and can argue their case with alacrity. There's nothing wrong, I ate earlier; I'm fine, don't worry for nothing.

And then there are the instincts of families, friends and loved ones which seem at odds with the illness too. The drive is to protect this frail and vulnerable person, or try to shock them into a true understanding, make them see the folly of their ways. Even our most simple words and greeting can be taken as a barb. 'You look well' is a knife in the heart of someone with anorexia. It means I must be fat, I knew it, I was right all along; I must rank up my efforts to restrict; I can't, I mustn't eat today.

It is little wonder that people with an eating disorder are often described (even in the medical literature) as deceitful, manipulative and unwilling to admit to their problems. The illness drives behaviour that can readily be interpreted in those pejorative terms. But it's not the truth, it's not how it's experienced from the inside and it's not helpful to anyone.

When an eating disorder strikes, it can seem to come out of nowhere. Model children who never gave their loving parents a moment's worry turn into screaming, scheming monsters as their very being gets subsumed into the illness. How did this happen? Where did we go wrong? Why didn't we see what was happening before our eyes? We must be awful parents.

Research is helping us to understand that the illness has much more of a biological basis than was ever thought to be the case before. Genetics, brain structure and brain chemistry are all implicated. Our brains and genes are more 'plastic' and adaptive, more influenced by their environment than we knew until recently. Epigenetics – the interplay of genes and environment – is a fascinating field of inquiry for researchers in many domains, including eating disorders.

Helping people with eating disorders understand the biological science behind their illness does a great deal to overcome any sense of stigma or shame for many. They didn't choose this illness. It isn't their or anyone else's fault. It isn't attention seeking or a cry for help. It isn't a silly fad or a phase. It's a serious, treatable condition. Being about brains, biology and genes does not mean it's a predetermined fait accompli. It's complex – a set of vulnerabilities, each of which raise the index of risk for an individual.

The medical profession finds the eating disorder condition baffling and overwhelming, too – and that includes those with specialist expertise in the illness. An eminent UK psychiatrist, Professor Hubert Lacey, recently retired, said: 'I know something about which treatments work for eating disorders, but faced with an individual patient – I know nothing about what will work for them.'

Few generalists have had any training on the topic and fewer still feel equipped to adequately support or treat someone with an eating disorder.

These patients are scary. They won't accept they are ill, don't do what they are told, lie to our faces and die on you. Helping clinicians understand the language of eating disorders – helping them see how the experience of having an eating disorder underpins and drives the actions they see – will improve treatment and care.

And as compassionate understanding grows and spreads among the eating disorder treatment world, then the hope of recovery and the belief in life without Ed will grow too. Bring it on.

*Susan Ringwood*

*Chief Executive*
*Beat*
*www.b-eat.co.uk*

# Index